MAF

Jill Duchess of Hamilton, former newspaper journalist in both Australia and Fleet Street, was born and educated in Sydney. She was sent to London as a correspondent for the Murdoch press in Australia. Assignments took her to America, India, Russia and Vietnam. In the late 1980s when living in France she started writing on Napoleon's family which led her both to the Hamilton archives in Scotland, and to the Duke of Hamilton and Brandon whom she married. She is co-author, among other books, of *The Flower Chain, The Gardens of William Morris* and *Scottish Plants for Scottish Gardens*. She has just completed *Napoleon, The Empress & The Artist*. Now divorced she lives in London and spends part of the year at her house on Magnetic Island in the Great Barrier Reef.

MARENGO

The Myth of Napoleon's Horse

Jill Hamilton

FOURTH ESTATE • *London*

This paperback edition published in 2001
First published in Great Britain in 2000 by
Fourth Estate
77–85 Fulham Palace Road
London W6 8JB
www.4thestate.co.uk

A catalogue record for this book is available from the British Library

ISBN 1-84115-352-4

Typeset by Avon DataSet Ltd, Bidford on Avon, Warwickshire
Printed in Great Britain by Clays Ltd, St Ives plc

*This book is a tribute
to all horses in all wars.
Memorials, after all,
can be in words as well as in stone.*

*Part of the royalties from the sale of this
book will go to The Home of Rest for Horses
in Buckinghamshire.*

*The author wishes to acknowledge the invaluable support
given by the Guards' Museum, London,
in researching this book.*

Napoleon's conquests.

Contents

Marengo's hoof on the dining table at the Officers' Mess, St James's Palace.

1

The Hoof at the Palace

A horse gives a man wings.

ALEXANDER THE GREAT

Every day when the Captain returns from the Changing of the Guard outside Buckingham Palace he sits down to lunch at a magnificent table set with gleaming regimental silver in the Officers' Mess. In front of him, in pride of place, is a horse's hoof. For over 150 years at St James's Palace this delicate but complete hoof, covered by a highly polished silver lid, has been moved between the sideboard and its central position above the knives and forks. Twenty-four words inscribed on the hinged lid link it with the man who was once Britain's most bitter enemy:

Hoof of Marengo, Barb charger of Napoleon, ridden by him at Marengo, Austerlitz, Jena, Wagram, in the campaign of Russia and lastly at Waterloo

Engraved on the underside of the lid is the story of how the hoof came into the Guards' hands:

Presented 8th April 1840 by J. W. Angerstein Captain Grenadier Guards and Lieutenant-Colonel to his brother officers of the Household Brigade

Today, Marengo's other two hooves are on public display with his preserved skeleton, a mile-and-a-half away, in the Waterloo Gallery at the National Army Museum in Chelsea. When Marengo died at the advanced age of thirty-eight in 1832 at Brandon in Suffolk, his bones were articulated by Surgeon Wilmott of the London Hospital. The skin was put aside for a taxidermist, but was lost or mislaid, as was his fourth hoof.

It seems fitting that in the Waterloo Gallery and the Guards' Mess the sole equine exhibit is from a horse belonging to Napoleon, whose military horsepower grew into the most remarkable cavalry force in history. In contrast, the cavalry was Wellington's least favourite military division. The British army horsemen went too fast, galloped at everything and lost control, so their performance during the Napoleonic Wars was not equal to that of the French. While Wellington's men and horses were first class, and the bravery of the officers was unquestioned, they lacked leaders with professional ambition. Although Napoleon's army was heavily dependent on infantry, his cavalry was a key to his army and helped to make it a gigantic weapon of conquest.

Of all Napoleon's horses, few could rival the later public role of Marengo. Since 1823, both dead and alive, he has been a star exhibit in Britain. The handbill advertising him when he first went on show in Pall Mall described him as a survivor of the Russian campaign. He was exhibited with 'the superb Saddle and Bridle and the Boots that Napoleon wore at Moscow'. Clear reminders of the thunder of battle were stressed:

He has five Wounds which are visible; and a Bullet still remains in his Tail. The Imperial Crown and the Letter N are branded on

his hind Quarters. He is so gentle, that the most timid Lady may
approach him without fear.

In England, where mighty Thoroughbreds were kings of the turf, the
fact that such an undersized steed could possibly have been the
personal mount of the once most powerful man in Europe came as a
surprise. Despite this drawback, Marengo had a great career in
England. The artist James Ward sold countless copies of a lithograph
romantically depicting him with rolling eyes and flared nostrils,
grieving for his deceased master as he looked out across the sea. This
engraving was issued as one of a series of four prints costing eight
shillings each and dedicated to George IV. The other horses were the
Duke of Wellington's beloved Copenhagen, George III's favourite
Adonis and a Cossack charger. The caption for Marengo's picture
read:

> The Portrait of Marengo, the favourite Barb-Charger rode by
> Napoleon Buonaparte at the Battle of Waterloo. The Property of
> Captain Howard (James Ward).

In the months after the Royal Academy opened its new exhibition of
painting on 26 May 1826, record crowds attended Somerset House.
One of the highlights was Ward's original painting of Marengo from
which the lithograph had been taken. By then, like Eclipse – who has
been called the greatest Thoroughbred racehorse of all time – and
many others to follow, Marengo had become a celebrity horse.

When his public show finished, Marengo was sold to a J. W.
Angerstein, who sent him to a stud farm at New Barnes in the Isle of
Ely in Cambridgeshire. Successful he might have been as a public
performer, but here he failed. He sired no notable racehorses, let
alone winners, although he was again brought to public notice,
appearing as 'Napoleon's Arabian' in the stud advertisements in the

3

Racing Calendar in 1825 and 1828 – services provided for a fee of ten guineas.

After he died, Marengo went on to have a long run as a war exhibit at the Royal United Service Institution (RUSI) Museum in Whitehall – Britain's first major war museum. When the museum was closed in 1962 most of the literature and exhibits were dispersed. The only catalogue now in the present library is the 1924 edition written by Sir Arthur Leetham. Extensive though the entry for Marengo is, it does not mention Captain Howard, referred to as the owner in the caption of the James Ward lithograph:

Skeleton of Marengo, Napoleon's favourite charger. Marengo was a light grey Barb, 14 hands one inch in height, and was procured by Napoleon in Egypt after the Battle of Aboukir in 1799. The horse was ridden by him at the Battle of Marengo, and named after the victory. It is believed subsequently to have carried his master at Austerlitz in 1805, at Jena in 1806, at Wagram in 1809, in the Russian Campaign of 1812, and at Waterloo in 1815, when he was wounded in the near hip. After Napoleon's defeat at Waterloo, Lord Petre gained possession of the horse and sold it to Lieut.-General J. J. W. Angerstein, who kept it at New Barnes, Ely, and bred from it. The animal was well cared for in his old age, and on his death his skeleton was given to this museum by Lieut.-General Angerstein [Angerstein was, in fact, Lieutenant-Colonel].

The decision of the RUSI to close its museum in 1962 might have ended Marengo's long appearance in London, but his success as a public exhibit ensured that he was transferred to the new National Army Museum when it opened in 1971. Today, beside his well-lit glass case, a notice almost duplicates the information in the RUSI catalogue, but adds that his hooves were made into snuffboxes and reduces his height to fourteen hands.

The 'lost' hoof of Marengo next to the larger hoof of a 16-hand hunter.

It is awesome to think that the horse in the Army Museum carried Napoleon in the Battle of Marengo in 1800 and fifteen years later at Waterloo; that right through the Napoleonic Wars this horse was ridden by the Emperor at the head of the most terrifying fighting force in Europe.

In recent history books, biographies and encyclopaedias on horses Marengo is still acknowledged as Napoleon's favourite charger. In his masterpiece *The Campaigns of Napoleon*, the military historian Dr David Chandler, formerly of the Royal Military Academy, Sandhurst, saluted his role: 'For short distances or on the battlefield the Emperor rode specially trained Arab horses (of which Marengo was the most famous).' In *The Animals' Who's Who*, published in London in 1982, Marengo is described as 'the white Arabian stallion who was Napoleon's favourite charger'.

Napoleon was an intrepid rider who usually rode stallions – even though they can be positively dangerous when bad-tempered. He galloped with a sense of daring and freedom unusual in someone so methodical. Even at breakneck speed, no obstacle worried him. The memoirs of his staff and courtiers show that on a horse

Napoleon feared little, while his attitude towards day-to-day stable welfare was often enlightened. He forbade his soldiers to dock the tails of their horses, a practice then prevalent in the British army, and horse-buyers were instructed to avoid purchasing horses with cut tails either for Napoleon or the French cavalry. Cropped tails saved effort in grooming, but a brush-like stump did not swish away troublesome flies and other insects, and also upset the horses' balance. In Britain this cruel custom was not banned until 1949.

As can be seen in Ward's painting, like most true Arabs, Marengo had a particular and beautiful way of carrying his tail, which, when walking, he always held to one side (either to the off or near) and elevated, unlike Thoroughbreds, which swing their tails from side to side when moving. Marengo's muscles were well developed and he must have been bold. As this description of Napoleon on horseback – from the *Mémoire* of Madame de Rémusat, lady-in-waiting to the Empress Josephine – shows, all horses ridden by Napoleon had to be both courageous and able:

He rode competently but without grace. Arabian horses were trained for him; he preferred them because they could stop suddenly. But as they also started suddenly, and as he held his bridle loosely, he would often have fallen if the necessary precautions had not been taken. He liked to gallop down steep slopes, at the risk of breaking the necks of those following him. He had several falls which were never mentioned, because it would have displeased him.

Another eye-witness account of Napoleon's regard for horses is given by Barry O'Meara, the Irish naval surgeon who accompanied Napoleon to exile on St Helena as his physician. His bestseller, *Napoleon at St Helena*, was devoured by the British public after its

Napoleon reviewing the Guard in the Palace du Carrousel, Paris,
by Horace Vernet.

publication in 1822. In it, he recorded Napoleon's thoughts and
showed the Emperor's deep understanding of horses:

> There is a link between animals and the Deity. Man is merely a
> more perfect animal than the rest. He reasons better. How do we
> know that animals have not a language of their own? . . . My
> opinion is that it is a presumption in us to say no, because we do
> not understand them. A horse has memory, knowledge, and
> love.

And when Napoleon talked of 'a horse', few readers doubted that he
was referring specifically to the battle-scarred animal which was now
part of the London scene, on show to all and sundry, and advertised

as 'Napoleon's favourite charger'. O'Meara, who had quarrelled with the Governor, Hudson Lowe, in 1818 and returned to England, was a strong supporter of Napoleon. He made a fortune from his memoirs, which, with their quotes from Napoleon, showing his sympathy for horses, touched a chord in the horse-loving British public. Napoleon praised his horse's excellent memory of places: 'When I lost my way, I was accustomed to throw the reins on his neck, and he always discovered places where I, with all my observation and boasted superior knowledge, could not.'

Impressed by the deference shown to Marengo by members of the British army, the Household Division and the National Army Museum, I decided to attempt to relate Marengo to Napoleon's life and battles. In doing so I hoped to find out why it was he, rather than the other horses in the imperial stables, who became an intrinsic part of the Napoleonic legend. In a curious way the fame of Napoleon was encapsulated by his white horses – and white horses have always been symbolic, near-mythical creatures, lending wings to man's imagination.

2

Napoleon's Early Years

Slave! I have set my life upon a cast,
And I will stand the hazard of the die.
I think there be six Richmonds in the field;
Five have I slain to-day, instead of him.
A horse! a horse! my kingdom for a horse!

WILLIAM SHAKESPEARE,
Richard III, Act V, Scene 4

[Napoleon] let his back slouch over the saddle, holding the reins loosely in his right hand, while the left arm hung free, all his body balancing to the horse's gait. He gave himself without reserve to the skill of his mount . . . let his horse go at a walk or a trot, content to be carried away in his thoughts; sometimes putting him to a gallop, he did not fear taking on difficult paths, marshy lowlands, or the slopes of rocks and ravines.

So wrote Napoleon's longest-serving secretary, Baron Fain. Napoleon did not have the figure, early aptitude or upbringing of a man who would become a fearless rider, transform the French cavalry and create six national studs, thirty stallion centres and three riding schools. During his childhood on the island of Corsica he never owned his own horse, nor was he tutored in equestrian skills. Although he acquired only a casual, practical attitude to riding as a child, he occasionally saw horses being used as regal and glamorous status symbols.

The only way of getting around the tracks on that mountainous island was on the back of a horse, a mule or donkey. The last two earned their keep as they were nimble, rarely collapsed from exhaustion or overloading and, while being able to carry heavy loads, ate less than horses. A normal day's ration for a horse was up to twelve pounds of hay, oats, bruised barley or Indian corn – and grass. The hilly terrain made it difficult to cultivate enough corn, hay, oats, straw and barley to feed large animals. The Bonaparte family sometimes rode through the pine forests to their olive groves and vineyards, the fields where they kept flocks of sheep and their farm at Villa Milelli, where they spent a few months each summer. But in the port of Ajaccio, where they spent most of the year, they did not have stables. Although the family were always hard up, they had an excellent library and old bills show that they spent large sums on fine clothes. But none on fine horses.

Napoleon Bonaparte was born in 1769 with a large head and sturdy body, but spindly legs. His head seemed too big for his body. At first his health was fragile, but he grew into an energetic child – despite a persistent hacking cough. Local boys nicknamed him 'Ribulione' (the troublemaker) as he was frequently brawling with them.

When Napoleon rode, his mounts were usually a borrowed donkey or mule, or, if he was lucky, the most hardened pony – anything a child with a puny frame could climb on. His mother later recounted how when he was seven and a half the family bailiff brought to their house two young and spirited horses. Napoleon mounted one of them, and, to the terror of every one, galloped off to the farm, laughing at their fright. The farmer brought him back.

When he was twenty Napoleon wrote, 'I was born when my country was dying.' Eighteenth-century Corsica was a wild and dangerous place. For over four centuries the Genoese had ruled it, exploiting the family blood-feuds which had made the island famous for its vendettas. To gain their independence, in 1755 the nationalists chose the bear-like Pasquale Paoli as their leader. Uniting the clans, Paoli drove the Genoese back into the coastal towns and became the virtual ruler for thirteen years, governing most of the island and even establishing a university at Corte. His fame rested on the unique democratic constitution which he drew up and which was acclaimed by leaders of the Enlightenment, from Rousseau and Voltaire to Hume and Frederick the Great.

James Boswell, the Scottish man of letters, made a pilgrimage to Corsica in 1765 and described the grandeur of riding on a magnificently saddled Corsican horse:

> One day when I rode out I was mounted on Paoli's own horse with rich furniture of crimson velvet, with broad gold lace, and had my guards marching along with me. I allowed myself to indulge a momentary pride in this parade, as I was curious to experience what could really be the pleasure of state and distinction with which mankind are so strangely intoxicated. When I returned to the Continent after all this greatness, I used to joke with my acquaintance and tell them that I could not bear to live with them, for they did not treat me with a proper respect.

Corsica was coveted by the French and the English because of its strategic significance in the Mediterranean – as well as being valued for its forests of tall, straight pines, which made good ships' masts. When the Genoese were beaten by the continual struggle against Paoli, they ceded the island to the French. The daring guerrilla war which followed could not save Corsican liberty. Finally, in June 1769,

Paoli boarded a British ship with 300 followers. He advised those who stayed, including his secretary, Carlo Bonaparte, to make peace with the French. Carlo's wife, Letizia, who had been hiding in the hills with one-year-old Joseph, returned to the family home in Ajaccio only three months before the birth of Napoleon.

After thirteen years of virtual independence the island slowly came to terms with French rule. Carlo Bonaparte, who had capitulated grudgingly, became an assessor in the law courts and, in 1777, the representative of the Corsican nobility at the court of Louis XVI in Versailles. Large subsidies were given to him for a mulberry tree plantation. Meanwhile the Bonaparte children were being brought up to regard the absent Paoli as a hero.

Despite Letizia's dowry and a few inheritances, Carlo had neither the land nor the money to achieve the position in society to which the family aspired – even with the help of the French governor of the island, the ageing but seductive Comte de Marbeuf, whose long-standing friendship with Letizia was so close that it was assumed they were having an affair. Teaching her son the value of keeping up appearances, *bella figura*, Letizia once said, 'It is more important to have a beautiful salon, a beautiful uniform, a horse to give an impression of wealth, even if one must eat dry bread at home.'

By the age of nine the patriotric Napoleon was openly anti-French, yet he received a state scholarship to attend a military academy in mainland France. Enrolled at the ancient school in Autun in Burgundy, the Italian-speaking 'Napoleone' was transferred six months later to the Military College, run by Franciscans, at Brienne, in the present-day department of Aube in the cold, windswept Champagne country. Later, he recalled with nostalgia a tree near the school, where 'when I was but twelve years old, I used to sit during play-hours and read'. A voracious reader, this solitary boy filled over 400 pages of notebooks with thoughts on many books, including those by Jean Jacques Rousseau, the Swiss philosopher who had risen

A sentimentalised depiction of Marengo by James Ward, 1823.

to fame in 1762. Napoleon's passion for history, for finding similarities in present events with those in the past, would stay with him all his life. He had a fascination with Alexander the Great, the Romans and the caliphs of Egypt, as well as with Alexander's campaigns in the Orient. This taught him the importance of cavalry in battle. He was especially interested that Gustavus Adolphus in the Thirty Years War followed the same strategy in battle as Alexander, Hannibal and Julius Caesar.

During six years at Brienne, Napoleon received only one visit from his parents and he never went home. Outings and opportunities to ride were few. Within the school grounds, though, students were encouraged to take up healthy outdoor recreation and Napoleon dug and planted a garden. Pining for the hidden caves and grottoes in which he used to hide in Corsica, he turned his little patch into a private haven where he could escape from people to read and meditate. He planted thick hedges to make safe green walls behind which he could, in complete privacy, along with more studious works, enjoy reading Rousseau's romantic novel, *La Nouvelle Héloise*, the book which had brought a return to nature into vogue. Napoleon's physical need for solitude would later be found on horseback when he would allow his horse to walk or trot, simply carrying him along – the lone rider lost in thought.

Having grown up beside the sea and being now deprived of it, and remembering, as only a child can, the real or imaginary adventures of the sailor husband of his wet-nurse, Camilla Ilari, his ambition became to pursue a career in the navy. During her only visit to the school, Napoleon's mother was horrified to find that her son, like other boys planning a naval career, slept in a hammock.

In October 1784 Napoleon swapped his austere cell-like room at Brienne for grander accommodation at the Ecole Militaire, in Paris, with its aristocratic traditions, regal stables and well-bred horses. Here he had his first taste of living in style. The Ecole Militaire, with its lavish Corinthian columns and squared, flattened dome, was founded by Louis XV at the suggestion of Madame de Pompadour. Since its completion in 1770 it had given officers a good general education, including Latin and foreign languages, but was limited to boys from families with a claim to nobility.

Although he was good at mathematics, geography and history, Napoleon was not an ideal student. His spelling was often phonetic; his handwriting was sometimes difficult to understand; he sneaked books into the German class, which he found boring, and exchanged surreptitious kicks under the desk with Louis Edmond le Picard de Phélippeaux. Their mutual loathing was so strong that in Abel Gance's classic 1927 film *Napoléon*, Phélippeaux is seen putting stones into the snowballs he intends to throw at the future Emperor. Napoleon spent his free time studying and writing. Apart from fencing and reading, his diversions were few. The lack of money was a hindrance, as it always had been.

He still wanted to go to sea. This, and his longing for independence, motivated him at the age of fifteen, to apply to accompany Jean François Galaup de la Pérouse on his expedition to the South Seas. Alexandre Jean des Mazis, Napoleon's schoolfriend, wrote the following about Napoleon's application:

> [Bonaparte] was in the mathematics class ... Messrs Dagelet and Monge ... our teachers ... sought and were granted the favour of joining as astronomers ... Buonaparte would have liked this opportunity of displaying his energy in such a fine enterprise, but Darbaud was the only one selected; they could not accept a greater number of pupils, and so Darbaud sailed.

After this refusal, with the help of a master, Napoleon wrote to the Admiralty in England requesting a place at the naval college in Portsmouth. Although the correspondence does not exist in the Public Record Office, the fact is known because Napoleon showed his letter to an English boy in the school, Robert Lawley from Shropshire, who was later created Baron Wenlock. Added to this disappointment was sorrow at the death of his father, who had died from stomach cancer.

Riding was still not a priority for Napoleon. Although students and horses were tutored in the traditional dressage methods of the school at Saumur, founded in the reign of Louis XV, Napoleon, it seems, did not greatly benefit from them. Beginners were supposed to be given three classes of equestrian instruction per week, but it is uncertain whether Napoleon took advantage of this. Whatever the case, the chief riding instructor stated that a minimum of three years was needed to make a cadet into a 'cavalier'. As Napoleon took his final exams a year early, he was only at the Ecole Militaire for a year and one week, so even if he had taken lessons he would not have had enough time – let alone patience – to improve his rough and ready riding techniques.

Des Mazis, who was graded fifty-sixth out of fifty-eight, wrote about the preparation for their examination in August 1785. Phélippeaux beat Napoleon by one place, forty-first to Napoleon's forty-second, and it was Phélippeaux, and not Napoleon, who was

Sketch of Napoleon by Jacques Louis David (1748–1825).

promoted to Second-Lieutenant. 'Cadet de Buonaparte' was passed in a final examination by Pierre Simon Laplace, the mathematician, astronomer and physicist who formulated the fundamental differential equation which bears his name. Later he headed the Académie des Sciences and became a lifelong friend to Napoleon.

On graduation Napoleon's commission in the artillery was signed personally by Louis XVI. While the cavalry was the most elite corps and the most snobbish, the artillery and the engineers were at the bottom of the social scale. Napoleon and des Mazis joined the La Fère regiment, then stationed at Valence on the River Rhône in the south of France and therefore not far from Corsica. After spending three months as an officer-cadet, he became an artillery officer in one of the four bombardier companies. As well as receiving intensive artillery training, he attended classes in mathematics, fortification, chemistry and physics, but had no equestrian training. Saddle horses were not available for all officers. However, Napoleon and des Mazis wanted to ride one day and, still dressed in their blue officer's uniforms, hired a couple of old horses. Much to the astonishment of onlookers, once the horses changed their canter into a fast gallop, the two men could not rein them in and they bolted through the village, hair and manes flying, returning to Valence at the same reckless pace. It took the two friends several days to recover.

This pattern of risk-taking and stretching physical endurance was a lifelong trait, as was Napoleon's inability to acquire the finer arts of horsemanship. But he knew he was a competent rider and had no time for the frills. He had the same attitude to deportment and dancing, other arts considered necessary for a gentleman and officer. He could not be bothered with the details. However, he had one skill few gentlemen of the time excelled at, swimming.

Napoleon's income was not large. Most of his salary went to help his widowed mother raise his four brothers and three sisters. He kept only enough to pay his landlady and buy his much-needed supply of books, paper, ink and quills. He seemed to have a pen in his hand more often than a sword. An aspiring writer, he wrote essay after essay: one was a tale about an idealistic young Corsican; another showed his passion for his native island; the most important were essays on Corsican freedom. He also started to write a history of Corsica. Paoli was still his hero and the freedom of Corsica was still his goal. Late into the night and before sunrise, he penned memorable aphorisms, such as, 'Men of genius are meteorites destined to burn, to light up their century.'

When he was given leave by his regiment to return to Corsica, he had spent all his money on books, so des Mazis lent him his fare.

17

Napoleon carried two valises, the smaller full of clothes, the larger full of books including translations of the classics – Plutarch, Plato, Cicero, Cornelius Nepos, Livy, Tacitus – plus Montaigne, Montesquieu, the Scottish bard Ossian and the memoirs of Rousseau's mistress, Madame de Warrens.

On 15 September 1786 Napoleon was once again 'on his native soil seven years and nine months after departure, at the age of seventeen years and one month'. He felt very nationalistic, very Corsican. Despite his French education, his French uniform with its blue and red coat, and his role as recruiting officer for the French army, he became embroiled in local politics and plans to liberate the island from that selfsame army. He managed to stay in Ajaccio for nearly a year – until 12 September 1787. Thereafter his long absences in Corsica repeatedly jeopardised his position in the French army. Between his first arrival in September 1786 and June 1793 he spent three-and-a-half years on his native island – often stirring up trouble. In seven-and-a-half years of service he spent just thirty months with his corps on the mainland. Although he used them to get around, during this period Napoleon had little to do with horses, let alone cavalry, both of which would soon be of great significance to him on the battlefield.

By the time Napoleon returned to the mainland, the La Fère regiment had moved from Valence to Auxonne. Napoleon now pushed himself to the maximum. Eating only one decent meal a day, at three p.m., he slept in a room with bare walls, with a bed, two chairs and a table covered with books and papers as his only furniture. After retiring at ten at night to save candles, he found time to write and study by rising at dawn. In the adjoining room his young brother Louis slept on a coarse mattress. Without a horse, Napoleon was forced to cover long distances on foot, often over twenty miles each morning to where his regiment was stationed. After a frugal breakfast he would walk to the garrison, arriving before noon, and sometimes going even further to check the proofs of his latest political pamphlet at the printers.

On 14 July 1789 a Paris mob stormed the Bastille, the symbol of power of the 1,300-year-old French monarchy. When told of its fall, the King exclaimed: 'Why this is a revolt', only to be corrected: 'No, sire, it is a Revolution!' The French Revolution overthrew the old order and plunged Europe into the most far-reaching crisis it had ever known. The new National Assembly declared the right of all citizens to liberty and equality – and Rousseau's *Contrat Social*, with its ringing phrases, 'Man is born free; and everywhere he is in chains', became the bible of the Revolution. The King and Queen were virtual prisoners in the Tuileries, the royal palace in central Paris. Emigrés started pouring into England from France, including many of the aristocratic graduates from the Ecole Militaire, two of them being des Mazis and Phélippeaux.

While most Corsican nationalists felt that the downfall of the old autocratic regime was the signal to throw off French rule, others, such as Christophe Saliceti, a lawyer and passionate revolutionary, believed that the island could be both independent and French. Saliceti proposed this in a debate at the National Assembly, which smoothed the way for Paoli's return. Parisians flocked to see the sixty-five-year-old revolutionary hero, who was presented to both the National Assembly and the King. Cries of 'Vive Paoli!' followed him as he travelled south to Corsica, where every village was *en fête*.

The fire, though, had gone out of Paoli after two decades of comfortable exile. A generous pension from the English parliament and good dinners with men such as Dr Johnson had, according to Napoleon, made him fat, white and like an Englishman. Paoli was at first favourably disposed towards the Bonapartes but not enough to help Napoleon with his research into the history of Corsica by letting him have copies of documents in his possession. However, he did offer him a job in the British army, as the wife of Rear-Admiral Sir Pulteney Malcolm reported:

The Admiral requested to know if it was true that he [Bonaparte] was offered a commission in the English army. He replied: 'I will tell you how it was. Paoli urged me to enter into the English service, he then had the power of procuring me a commission as high a rank as I could expect; but I preferred the French, because I spoke the language, was of their religion, understood and liked their manners, and I thought the beginning of a revolution a fine time for an enterprising young man.'

If Napoleon had gone to England, his lack of style in horsemanship would have counted against him. Despite their skill at dressage and stag and boar hunts, the French did not share the English tradition of riding horses for sport. In England foxhunting was often a young man's main preparation for battle. The thrusting, hell-for-leather pace that both men and horses learnt galloping at great speed over rough country in pursuit of a fox was reflected on the battlefield. The British cavalry charged with tremendous dash, but in their enthusiasm they often lost control of the situation, a fault Napoleon and Wellington both noted later and one which almost gave Napoleon victory at Waterloo.

Napoleon decided against leaving Corsica, which was in political turmoil. The cause of Corsican separatism was dividing the island and three groups were emerging – Royalist, National (Paoli) and Popular (Republican). In one brief struggle Napoleon was found fighting with volunteers against French troops, but the episode was so muddled that he escaped court martial. A report of the incident sent to the Ministry of Justice in Paris gathered dust in the confusion following the Revolution.

In June 1791 the King, Marie Antoinette and their children, heavily disguised, attempted to flee France in a carriage. But they were arrested at Varennes and returned to Paris. From then onwards in Corsica, as throughout France, the monarchy became ever more unpopular and Republicanism gained ground.

After the French army authorities discovered that Napoleon was absent without leave in Corsica, he went to Paris in May 1792 to argue his case. On the morning of 20 June, when a large and violent mob entered the Tuileries and presented the King with a petition, Napoleon happened to be nearby. A noisy rabble of five to six thousand wrecked the elaborate formal garden as they surged inside. Humiliating the King, they forced him to put on a red Cap of Liberty and drink with them 'to the health of the Nation'. Eventually the King managed to calm them.

This frightening scene turned out to be the prelude to the Paris insurrection during a heatwave, on 10 August, which Napoleon also witnessed. With his old friend Louis Antoine Bourrienne he watched the events from a furniture shop in the carousel belonging to Bourrienne's brother. This time 30,000 people broke into the garden of the Tuileries, shouting 'Down with the King! Long live the nation!' Finding the royal family gone, the mob butchered the loyal Swiss Guard.

'*Si Louis XVI s'était montré à cheval, la victoire lui fût restée,*' Napoleon wrote to his brother Joseph. 'Had the king shown himself on horseback, he would have retained victory.' These were strange words indeed from a man who at that stage showed scant interest in anything equine and who was known to be a rough rider. Perhaps Napoleon was recalling the first anniversary of the storming of the Bastille when the day had belonged to General Lafayette because of his horse. There had been such a euphoric mood as people waited for the King but instead they saw Lafayette mounted on a beautiful white horse. Napoleon would use the power that a horse could confer on his rider to dominate situations and people throughout his life. In contrast to Napoleon, Louis XVI had been trained from childhood to be an expert rider; he looked and felt commanding on horseback, losing his usual awkwardness. He loved horses and was said to be able to list 118 horses which he had ridden.

Within weeks the King was thrown into the tower in the Temple prison; the French Republic was declared and the pace of revolution became more frenzied. The Republic was proclaimed in September 1792 and was followed by the thud of the guillotine. A new assembly (the National Convention) came into being and the King was condemned to death by a small majority in January 1793.

A few months later Napoleon was back in Corsica and quarrelling with Paoli. Napoleon's enthusiasm for Corsican nationalism was decreasing. He was coming to realise that Corsica was too small to be autonomous and would always be dominated by a stronger power. Where Paoli favoured English protection, Napoleon preferred the French. Apart from the brothers Bonaparte, few residents in Ajaccio could express themselves well in French although they had been under French rule for twenty-three years.

Napoleon's brother Lucien made a powerful speech at a political meeting in Toulon. Paoli, he said, was a traitor who was about to hand over the island to the English. Paoli was summoned to Paris to answer this and other complaints about his loyalty to the Republic. Using 'old age and broken health' as an excuse, he stayed in Corsica. At the same time opposition to Napoleon was growing among counter-revolutionaries, led by the young nobleman Carlo Pozzo di Borgo, who started a family vendetta against the Bonapartes. Five years older than Napoleon, he became one of his fiercest opponents. His supporters ransacked the Bonaparte family home in Ajaccio, declaring: 'it would be beneath the dignity of the Corsican nation to have anything more to do with them. Enough to abandon them to remorse and public execration.'

Napoleon's attempts to gather support failed and the islanders rose up against him. With the help of Saliceti and his brother, Joseph, he escaped on a borrowed horse and hid in the grotto of a friend's garden before managing to escape on a boat. A terrified Letizia, with her younger children, took to the hills. On the night of 3 June 1793 they made their way to the edge of the Campo d'Oro, now the site of the modern airport of Ajaccio. Napoleon swam ashore and rescued his family, getting them on board a merchant ship which then evaded the English patrols and reached the port of Toulon.

'*Cette fois – et pour toujours – Napoleon a choisi la France*' ('This time – and forever – Napoleon has chosen France'), wrote the French historian André Castelot.

In February 1794 12,000 British troops invaded the island. In bitter fighting against the French, Admiral Nelson's right eye was badly injured in an 'explosion of stones'. The British ruled the island for two years and George III was proclaimed King of Corsica. Paoli and Pozzo di Borgo now worked for the English.

In France the Terror was reaching its peak. Arrests and executions were frequent in Toulon and chaotic conditions forced the Bonapartes to move to cheap rooms in Marseilles. For a while Letizia sent her two eldest high-spirited daughters, Pauline and Marianne (later Elisa), to work as laundresses. The third daughter, Caroline, was only twelve.

In 1793 Napoleon's work involved both riding and organising horses. Rejoining the 4th Artillery regiment, he managed to obtain his back pay – most of which went to his mother and to settle a printer's bill. He was ordered to accompany horse-drawn convoys of powder wagons between Nice and Marseilles. His spare time was spent writing. Urged on by Saliceti, he wrote a pamphlet, *Le Souper de Beaucaire*, which attacked Paoli as a traitor and argued for united action by all Republicans. Saliceti, now a political commissar, was more than useful to the Bonapartes. He helped Joseph Bonaparte obtain a good post; applied to Paris for compensation for the Bonaparte family; and showed Napoleon's pamphlet to Augustin Robespierre, the brother of Maximilien, the leader of the twelve-man executive in Paris. Napoleon's next break again came through Saliceti's influence. While the convoy was passing through Toulon, Napoleon was removed from it and was appointed to take the place of a wounded artillery commander.

'The beginning of my rise was at [the Battle of] Toulon,' said Napoleon. 'The artillery in which I was serving was badly officered, a number had been privates without education. It was known to the general that I had been well educated at the Ecole Militaire.'

This was Napoleon's opportunity to go into action against the English. Royalist rebels in Toulon, France's chief naval base and arsenal on the Mediterranean, had revolted against the Reign of Terror and allowed an Anglo-Spanish fleet commanded by Admiral Hood into the port. During the siege, which lasted for three months, the number of English and Spanish troops increased to 15,000. The Republicans feared that the revolt would escalate to defeat the Republic, especially now that Marie Antoinette had been executed.

Napoleon had his first chance to show off his inventive use of surprise tactics based on manoeuvrability and speed. At last his feet were well and truly in the stirrups. Setting off at a gallop, and followed by a hundred cavalrymen, he was everywhere. He enticed Hood to bring his ships closer into port. Four days of battle, in a terrible downpour which drenched the men and threatened to spoil the gunpowder, followed. At one stage Napoleon even ordered a charge. Though wounded in the thigh, he did not stop. Three horses were killed under him. When there was no ammunition left, hand-to-hand fighting with cold steel began. The English gunners were hacked to pieces. As the last British defences were crumbling, the indomitable Sir William Sidney Smith, a Captain in the Royal Navy who had distinguished himself as a midshipman, gave the order to pour oil and pitch over the decks and fuses of the French ships and arsenal. Much of the French fleet was set ablaze. Napoleon later remembered the horror of the fire:

The whirlwind of flames and smoke from the arsenal was like the eruption of a volcano, and the thirteen vessels blazing in the roads were like thirteen magnificent displays of fireworks . . . an unparalleled spectacle. The French were torn to the heart to see

24

such great resources and so many riches consumed in so short a time.

On 17 December the British evacuated the port and two days later the French regained control of Toulon. Napoleon struck up a friendship with Augustin Robespierre, the commissioner to the army, who wrote to his brother Maximilien praising the 'transcendent merit' of Napoleon, who was promoted from Captain to Brigadier-General. One of his new supporters was the *représentant en mission* with the army, Vicomte Paul François Nicolas de Barras, first cousin to the infamous Marquis de Sade. This friendship led to Napoleon's meteoric rise in the army, his marriage – and to Barras's downfall. Because of the part he had played at Toulon and his pamphlet, Napoleon was ideologically acceptable to members of the revolutionary government and was entrusted with a diplomatic mission to Genoa. But in July 1794 he was swept up in the backlash against Robespierre. Robespierre had attained the height of his power, but when he condemned the leading revolutionary Georges Danton to death for conspiracy against the Republic, public reaction against this and his other ruthless policies grew. Augustin Robespierre was guillotined and his brother Maximilien executed.

Although the fury of the Revolution had now spent itself, Napoleon was imprisoned at Fort Carré near Antibes under suspicion of being a terrorist. After two weeks locked up with nothing to read but a book on Roman law, he was released through the influence of Saliceti, his old friend and mentor who had, for some unclear reason, caused him to be put in prison in the first place. In Paris a woman from Martinique, soon to become Barras's mistress and then Napoleon's wife, was ending her four months' imprisonment in the old convent of the Carmelites with its damp and blood-stained walls. Five days before Robespierre's career was ended, the head of her husband, Alexandre, Viscount Beauharnais, although a Revolutionary, had fallen under the guillotine.

Portrait of Napoleon by Antoine-Jean Gros, 1803.

Continuing his pattern of going to Paris when there was a crisis or gap in his life, Napoleon arrived there at the end of 1794. With not enough francs in his shabby military coat and his sallow skin pale from years of poverty, he found rooms in the Marais with his friend Androche Junot, who would later be one of his top generals. After a few months Napoleon was appointed to a position by the Committee of Public Safety on the recommendation of his friend Barras, who was soon to become a member of the Directoire. Five *directeurs* would hold supreme power, responsible to two legislative bodies, the Council of the Ancients and the Council of Five Hundred.

Napoleon was on his way. However, despite his grand friendships, not for another year, after 5 October 1795, could he claim to have arrived. On that day 20,000 well-armed Royalists marching to the city centre were thwarted by Napoleon. With the help of his new friend, Joachim Murat, he placed 4,000 men in a protective circle around the Tuileries and, ordering a 'whiff of grapeshot', blasted the insurgent crowds. He mowed down the rebels under a barrage of fire, killing around 1,400, but preserving France from further anarchy. Leaving his depressing room in the Marais district Napoleon moved to better lodgings and was soon to be seen riding in a carriage.

Murat, artistic, tall and good-looking and recognizable by his flamboyant uniforms, was one of the thousands of men who benefited from the Revolution. The son of a Gascon innkeeper, he started life as a stable boy. In the old army he would never have risen above the rank of sergeant; in the Revolutionary army he rose to lead its most elite division, the cavalry. Napoleon's faith in Murat was so remarkable that he arranged his marriage, when he was thirty-four, to eighteen-year-old Caroline Bonaparte, then still at boarding school. Murat and Napoleon were linked by their common love of horses and cavalry. Murat, leading his famed Cavalry Reserve to glory, would eventually become Commander of the Garde des Consuls, Governor of Paris and finally a Marshal and King of Naples.

For Napoleon, money, mistress and celebrity followed. On the strength of his knowledge of mathematics and science, he was invited to attend the newly-formed Institut National, the revamped Académie des Sciences. More significantly, he was raised to the rank of Artillery Divisional General at the insistence of Barras, who ensured that his

*Napoleon attacking rebel Royalists in Paris on 5 October 1795
(13 Vendémiaire).*

protégé took his place when he resigned as Commander-in-Chief of
the Army of the Interior. Napoleon even took over Barras's discarded
mistress, Rose de Beauharnais. With Madame Tallien and Madame
Récamier she led Parisian society. Her popularity and her attachment
to Barras were more than useful to a twenty-six-year-old ambitious
general. On their first night together he nicknamed her Josephine. A
member of a group known as Les Merveilleuses, 'the marvellous
ones', she was admired for her daringly sheer white muslin dresses,
with high waists, short puffed sleeves and bodices which pushed up
her breasts, revealing a bold cleavage. A later satirical cartoon by the
English caricaturist James Gillray showed her with her friend Madame

Tallien dancing naked before Barras, while a startled General Bonaparte peered at the scene through a gauze curtain.

By his own admission, Napoleon had been shy in the presence of women before he met Josephine. Despite her pretensions to aristocracy, she skilfully convinced the Revolutionary government of her loyalty and she was accepted in all levels of Paris society. She became

Sketch of Napoleon by Jacques Louis David (1748–1825).

Napoleon's link between the *ancien régime* and the new revolutionary class.

Two and a half weeks after their wedding banns were published in Paris in mid-February 1796, Napoleon was made Commander of the army in Italy. As Josephine was still close to Barras it was said that the promotion was given as 'Josephine's dowry'. Barras himself was one of the witnesses at the wedding ceremony. Josephine falsified the dates on the marriage certificate to make it seem that Napoleon was older than she was, instead of six years younger. With the excuse that she could not procure her birth certificate from Martinique, she gave the year of birth as 1763, a generous mistake; Napoleon used the certificate of his brother Joseph who was born in 1768.

3

Italy: Using Horses as Emblems of Power

We are heathen who worship an idol
We keep for our pleasure and pride
We are slaves of the saddle and bridle,
Yet kings of the earth when we ride!

W. H. OGILVIE,
'Kings of the Earth' (1913)

Within two days Napoleon's honeymoon was over and he was on a relay of horses heading south to fight Austria. France had been at war with the major monarchies on the continent for four years, but had now made peace with all of them – except Austria.

Arriving in Nice to take command of his army, Napoleon found 42,000 poorly equipped and dispirited men. Scattered from Nice to Savona, they were surrounded by enemies: on land the Austrian and Sardinian armies; at sea the British navy. Hood might have lost his foothold at Toulon, but he now had the advantage of a naval base in Corsica.

Although he was looked upon as an upstart by more experienced French generals, Napoleon managed to placate them and to raise the spirits of the ragged troops. After drummers sounded the reveille he shouted:

Soldiers! You are naked and ill-fed. The Government owes you much, but it can give you nothing . . . I want to lead you into the most fertile plains in the world. Rich provinces and great towns will be in your power. There you will find honour, glory and riches.

Two hours later the troops were marching. Napoleon, leading men and horses to victory after victory, pushed eastwards. His success shook Europe to its foundations and he became the hero of the French Republic. 'People of Italy,' he proclaimed, 'the Army of France has broken your chains.' Soon millions of francs, vast stores of provisions, thousands of horses and art treasures were ceded to France in lieu of war taxes. The Italians were learning the cost of freedom.

Now the time had come to show that horses were emblems and a source of power. Riding in triumph to enter Milan on 15 May, Napoleon alighted from his coach before the city entrance and mounted a pale grey horse called Bijou. At a steady pace, followed by 500 cavalry and to the sound of stirring regimental music, he made the entrance of a conqueror into the city. Using his mount to elevate himself, his entry was described as being more like that of a monarch than a Republican general. Wonderfully accoutred horses and men, martial music and regimental flags would be a feature of his ceremonial occasions for the next nineteen years.

Slouched forward, legs pointing downwards so the tips of his toes were lower than the heels – Napoleon did not cut a fine figure on a horse. His relaxed attitude was far from the classical position, which requires a straight body with the ball of the foot in the stirrup and the heel well down. As the casual Corsican way of riding was without bits in the animal's mouths, the reins were kept loose and the rider steered by exerting pressure on the animal's neck. Napoleon had a straight leg position and directed the horse by using shifts in bodyweight rather than depending on a mouthpiece. Like most men who learnt to ride with primitive bridles without iron bits, Napoleon's control over the horse involved a near symbiosis with the animal, following his rhythm instinctively.

Napoleon thought horsepower so important that he took personal control of all mounted units. According to Count Caulaincourt, who would later become his Master of the Horse, after whom the road beside the cemetery in Montmartre is named, Napoleon 'seemed to extract men, horses and guns from the bowels of the earth!' – despite the perpetual shortage of good horses in France. The emigration of Royalist officers and the land-owning aristocracy during the Revolution had deprived the French cavalry of men, mounts and fine breeding stock. As the centuries-old social structure changed and aristocrats fled across the Rhine or over the Channel, their horse studs deteriorated. Despite protests from statesmen like Mirabeau, who had studied horses in England, stud farms were shut and stallions sold off. They were a particular target because finely bred horses were associated with wealth, privilege and excess. To compensate for this deficiency in good breeding stock, Napoleon drained conquered countries of their horses, resurrected the stallion depots and gradually developed fine Arab breeding stock. But Napoleon's personal choice in horses was not shared by his contemporaries. His little Arabs did not have the same wide appeal as Thoroughbreds.

Napoleon's demands for horseflesh knew no bounds as is seen from this letter of 14 June 1796 from French headquarters in Tortona, complaining that excessive requisitioning of horses and bullocks was imposing a burden on the population:

> Citizen Quartermaster, complaints are reaching the Commander-in-Chief from all sides as to the burden being placed on the unhappy people of the conquered country by the requisitioning of horses and bullocks by the transport contractor. It is said that simple employees go to the length of imprisoning officials and the misery of the poorest people around Mantua is such that they are inclined to emigrate with all their beasts.

Napoleon could be ruthless, even with his horses. Despite his dependence on them, the urgency of battle meant that he made impossible demands. Like many military men, he could appear indifferent to a sea of corpses on a battlefield, but instances of deliberate cruelty on his part were rare. Yet in January 1797 with a high fever and so ill that he could hardly stand, he raced day after day, pushing himself on to Verona, where another battle was to be fought. Three horses died of exhaustion under him.

Using a high percentage of horsemen in an army was then controversial. While most military leaders believed that horses were essential for reconnaissance purposes, for officers' mobility and for the merciless pursuit of the enemy after battle, some commanders considered it wasteful to pit cavalry against modern weaponry, and especially against infantry squares, unless it too was supported by enough infantry. Horses and cavalry needed expert leadership. Not only was cavalry expensive because of the cost of purchasing and maintaining horses, but it required more officers than infantry and the men needed more instruction. If a horse failed, the man in the saddle was next to useless. Sabre and bayonet cuts around the head and neck became major causes of death, as were wounds from gun and grapeshot. A soldier on horseback was a massive target and the introduction of mightier firearms made any mounted man much more vulnerable than he would have been in the late seventeenth century.

Napoleon's army forced back the Austrian troops until the Peace of Campo Formio ended Austrian participation in the War of the First Coalition in October 1797. It gave France control over northern Italy and Belgium. That Britain remained France's sole enemy was evident constantly as shortages and surpluses caused by trade embargoes became part of everyday life in both countries.

Napoleon returned from Italy triumphant on 5 December to a Paris thronged with rejoicing crowds. Sentinels had difficulty in keeping back the people outside his house in rue Chantereine, which had been renamed rue de la Victoire in his honour. Rented by Josephine when she had been widow de Beauharnais, it had been purchased by Napoleon after their marriage and redecorated at huge expense. Among the waiting mail was a sinister and prophetic letter from Sir William Sidney Smith, the mercurial naval captain who had faced Napoleon at Toulon. He had been captured attempting to raid Le Havre and was charged with trying to burn the port, as he had the dockyard at Toulon, and was known to be an intelligence officer as well as a naval officer. It was on the wooden shutter of the gloomy Temple prison, the last abode of both Louis XVI and Marie Antoinette, that Smith wrote a letter taunting Napoleon, predicting that the wheel of fortune would turn and that one day Napoleon himself would suffer reverses and be imprisoned. But Napoleon's old foe from school, Phélippeaux, now a Royalist agent, managed to release Smith by impersonating a police commissioner and producing a forged document. Phélippeaux, one of many aristocrats who had fled in 1791, had secretly slipped back into France to take part in counter-revolutionary activities.

The French government, in anticipation of invading England, made Napoleon Commander of the so-called 'Army of England'. The revolutionary wars had reached a stalemate, with France winning on land and Britain victorious at sea. Britain dominated world trade and would remain the one nation that Napoleon could not defeat. While every other major nation in Europe changed from being France's enemy, to its submissive ally, then back again to enemy, Britain never wavered – except during the brief Peace of Amiens in 1802–3.

In 1798 British naval supremacy made direct assault across the Channel out of the question. As an alternative, Napoleon proposed the invasion of Egypt and the Directoire agreed, partly because they wanted to get him out of the way – his popularity was a growing threat to their existence. The invasion could 'menace Britain's trade with the Indies and with India' and 'shake England to her marrow-bones' as well as expanding France's own dominions. At a meeting of the Institut de France which was attended by leading scientists of the Republic, Napoleon, who had been elected a member of the mathematical section, sought support to make the Egyptian expedition one of learning and science. He also planned to found a colony on the Nile. This area of northern Africa would become the platform for further far-flung expeditions such as a march to the Indus in the winter of 1801–2 with 60,000 men, 50,000 camels and 10,000 horses. Men, camels and horses were to be recruited locally.

Spies informed the English that an immense number of ships were gathering in French ports, but their destination was unknown. After waving goodbye to a tearful Josephine at Toulon on 19 May, Napoleon managed to evade the English fleet, then under Nelson's command. Installed in a beautifully appointed cabin on the mighty French flagship *L'Orient* – and accompanied by thirteen ships of the line, nine frigates and 232 transports – Napoleon sailed for Egypt via Malta.

On board the ships were 37,000 soldiers and 197 scientists and artists of the Scientific and Artistic Commission, but only 1,250 horses – just enough for the officers, a squadron of cavalry, and for pulling the 171 cannon. Most cavalrymen were equipped with harnesses and saddles – they would have to buy, borrow, steal or seize mounts on arrival. The lack of horses was due to limited space on the ships and the high death rate of horses at sea – there was on average a

25 per cent loss. Horses needed a minimum of ten times the space given to each soldier. Embarkation and disembarkation were also highly dangerous – especially when ships were unable to moor alongside a quay and the animals had to be swung on board with cumbersome pulleys, tackle and slings. Sometimes when disembarking, horses were lowered on slings into the water and left to swim ashore. Large animals were normally carried in the waists of ships along with the shipboard larder of penned-up pigs, sheep and hens.

Conditions at sea for animals were horrendous. Ships' quarters were claustrophobic and horses had to tolerate being tied down in slings with safety harness through rough seas. When waves tossed a ship on its side, horses broke bones easily or were cast down in their boxes – rolling so close to the wall that they could not get up. Inadequate food and water supplies on board often caused further troubles. The water available was usually no more than five gallons a day and horses normally drink between six to seven gallons, depending on the weather and their activity. On long voyages, semi-starvation caused mange. Colic was common.

Disposing of manure and other garbage was awkward for ships sailing clandestinely. Debris floating on the surface of the sea attracted birds and could lead to detection. Smells were also a setback. Ships in which the stables were not cleaned daily of stale dung and urine could be smelled by keen sailors miles away. Bad air irritated the mucous membranes of both men and horses and produced catarrh. The smells on board were a bane for anyone as sensitive to bad odours as Napoleon, whose sense of smell was so keen that he carried two phials of special cologne in his boots to mask the stench of the battlefield.

This was the first major sea voyage for the man who had wanted to be a sailor rather than a soldier. His huge armada arrived at Malta on 9 June, where the Knights of St John surrendered with little resistance. Three weeks later Napoleon landed in Egypt. Once he had 4,000 men ashore at Marabout Beach, eight miles west of Alexandria, he attacked the city. After defending their homes and mosques, killing 200 Frenchmen and wounding General Menou, who had been given a divisional command, with a well-aimed stone, the Egyptians capitulated. A week later, leaving armed ships in the harbour, General Kléber in charge of troops in Alexandria and Menou as Governor of the nearby port of Rosetta with a small garrison to keep the seaways secure, Napoleon led about 24,000 men – and some already requisitioned horses – towards Cairo. Issued with only a water bottle and four days' ration of biscuit, the men found the dry heat excruciating and the lack of shade an ordeal. In the desert the temperature soared to between 110 and 126 degrees Fahrenheit, leaving both men and horses semiconscious with thirst and exhaustion. Water was scarce and, since it seldom rains in Egypt, each man shared his pitiful water ration with his drooping horse. At the halts men squabbled over dirty puddles of water. Marauding Bedouin killed stragglers and at night fired at their bivouacs, causing the precious horses to stampede. Some horses went for days without a drink.

When a horse died, the soldier had to straggle behind on foot, carrying his own load as best he could, until, if lucky, he managed to claim the beast of a dead companion or kidnap a donkey or a camel in a village. Exhausted men walked distances which seemed immeasurable. Thirst made them see mirages of crystal-clear water on the horizon. At last, to their enormous relief, they found a field of melons growing on the banks of the Nile.

Cut off from mainstream Europe for centuries, Egypt was unprepared for the shock of French military strategy. In the sixteenth century the Sultan of the Ottoman Empire had made Egypt a Turkish province, entrusting it to the government of twenty-four Mameluke Beys. But over the centuries the Mamelukes' power had grown so much that they extended their control. Descended from slaves imported from the Black Sea and trained as soldiers, the Mamelukes had no concept of war other than a fast charge on horseback followed by quick combat. Prepared for fighting from childhood with their iron helmets, javelins, pistols and curved thrusting spears, they were strangers to the tactics of eighteenth-century warfare. They would charge with the reins clenched in their teeth, both hands clutching a sabre, savouring the exhilaration of the moment, as free and as fast as the wind.

The minarets of Cairo were sighted on 21 July – and so were 6,000 Mameluke horsemen. This resulted in the first pitched battle in which East and West had met since the Crusades. Called by Napoleon the Battle of the Pyramids, it was a contest between men trained in modern military tactics and those who still relied on an army with a tradition of finely bred horses. The Mameluke cavalry charged like a tornado, rending the air with hideous yells and discharging their firearms at full gallop. It is said that Napoleon was so impressed by the quality and beauty of the Arab chargers that he could hardly bear to give his artillery the order to fire on them.

Napoleon showed that even then he was an expert tactician where cavalry was concerned. He kept back a strong block of horses until the enemy was nearly exhausted, ready to aim at one point, then another. The Mameluke horsemen were not trained to move and fight in squadrons, they simply charged furiously in scattered groups. But Napoleon learnt from them. They were, he wrote, 'the finest cavalry in the world'.

Murat's assault against the Mamelukes brought him to prominence as the most dashing – and flashiest – cavalry leader in the desert. Always ready for excitement, his vanity and ambition knew few limits. Known as *le beau sabreur*, he was already a vital force in Napoleon's life, as was the fair-haired Victor Leclerc, the self-assured and daring heir to a flour merchant who had married Napoleon's favourite sister, Pauline, during the Italian campaign. He was also distinguished in the battle for his handling of horses. Both he and Murat led brilliant cavalry charges at the Battle of the Pyramids.

This battle, as planned, led to the capture of more horses – and to the fall of Cairo. Recalling Alexander's liberation of Egypt from the Persians more than 2,000 years earlier, Napoleon bellowed to his soldiers: 'From the height of these pyramids, forty centuries look down on you.' That night the French stripped the bodies and horses – taking jewels, gold, ornate saddles and stirrups said to be of pure copper, some of which weighed over twelve pounds. Much of what they plundered came from times long past.

The Egyptians had a fluid riding style like the one Napoleon had known as a child; it was more to his liking than the stiff formality and more exhibitionist French dressage. He was impressed by their horses and riding methods, and developed a special affinity with the cavalry in Egypt which would stay with him all his life. Seizing Egyptian horses was part of his long-term plan to improve French bloodlines and revitalise the depleted French studs and rundown cavalry schools. As he had in Italy, he acquired hundreds of fine remounts. It was imperative to sequester local saddle-horses for the cavalry units and pack animals for transport immediately. While some were captured in battle, in the areas of Alexandria, Giza and Qalyub many were forcibly requisitioned from the inhabitants under cruel threats. Every owner was paid an arbitrary price in which he had no say and, because of lack of ready money, only pieces of paper were issued, entitling owners to later reimbursement.

Napoleon, in the saddle, made a slow and triumphal entry into Cairo on 24 July 1798. When General Kléber received the news of the victory of the Battle of the Pyramids on 31 July in Alexandria, he fired salvoes of artillery and declared the day a public holiday. Leading citizens offered their congratulations. But then disaster struck.

Guesswork took Admiral Nelson and the British Mediterranean Squadron to the Egyptian port of Aboukir Bay, near the Rosetta mouth of the Nile, on 1 August. Nelson attacked and one of the bloodiest naval fights of all time, known as the Battle of the Nile, began. Once again the English set fire to the French ships – it was only five and a half years since they had burnt much of the French fleet at Toulon. Eleven of France's best ships of the line were destroyed. The battle was immortalised in the poem 'Casabianca' by F. D. Hemans about the twelve-year-old son of Captain Casabianca of the *L'Orient*, burnt to death, like so many that night, on his father's ship: 'The boy stood on the burning deck, Whence all but he had fled'. By a strange coincidence, a ship loaded with Maltese treasure was captured by an English frigate which would play a fateful part at the end of Napoleon's career, the 74-gun, twelve-year-old *Bellerophon*.

Napoleon's hopes of disrupting the British route to India and chasing England 'from all its possessions in the East' were sunk with his ships, while victory gave Nelson the title Baron Nelson of the Nile. The French now had no vessels in which to return to France. The British were determined to dislodge them from Egypt and blockaded the Egyptian coast – the sea was dotted with English sails. The high risk of mail being intercepted (although some packages got through via Tripoli and Tunis) by Royal Navy ships meant there was no safe way for Napoleon and his isolated army to communicate with France. The blockade was so successful that it also disrupted normal Egyptian import and export trade across the Mediterranean and even stopped coastal traffic between Alexandria, Rosetta and Damietta. Napoleon's attempt to import wine, brandy, raisins and timber from Corfu, then a French possession, came to nothing. Native merchants suffered, as did local captains and shippers. Blockades, like battles, were to become a major feature of Napoleon's life.

With over 30,000 troops bivouacked around the Pyramids, Napoleon, ignoring the heat, infections and desert maladies, let alone his naval defeat, undertook the administration and modernisation of Egypt. Under the direction of Nicolas Conté, the engineer, the first windmills ever to mill corn and raise water were introduced. Until then primitive mills had been driven by animal traction or by hand.

Even in the early twentieth century, windmills in Egypt were still known as 'Bonaparte's mills'. The 'sanitary committee' of Cairo made the city, especially its drains and canals, a little healthier and street lamps were placed at regular intervals. A bridge of boats was thrown between the two banks of the Nile. There were no roads then in Egypt

*Sketch of Napoleon by Jacques Louis
David (1748–1825).*

and surveys were started to create a network of highways to be used during the floods. Napoleon's reforms extended to trying to set up civilian hospitals and medical centres. An interest in medicine meant that French doctors in the expedition subsequently introduced cannabis into European medicine. Every effort was made to achieve a rapprochement between Christianity and the Muslim faith, and a point was made of not interfering with the all important religious month of Ramadan. As far as he could, Napoleon conformed to Muslim custom, receiving his guests according to their etiquette and sitting in their midst 'à la turque'. His greatest contribution, though, was to establish the foundations of Egyptology – including the study of the Pyramids, the Sphinx, Luxor, Karnak and the Rosetta Stone. When the stone was discovered all knowledge of the ancient Egyptian language and writing had been lost for over a thousand years. Napoleon ordered copies and impressions to be made of it so work could commence on deciphering the ancient Egyptian scripts. For the rest of his life he followed the work of the scholars and scientists who had accompanied him to Egypt.

Just as Napoleon was not bothered about the correct way to ride, so he was impatient and fidgety when talking to people. This direct Corsican manner, though, won him the loyalty of the common soldiers; he laughed and jested with them, haranguing them with a rough tenderness. Despite the difference of rank he displayed the air more of a student than a general. Familiarity between officers and men in the post-revolutionary French army was not unusual – relationships between ranks were less formal than in the British army. But even though every soldier could hope to reach the highest rung on the military ladder, only a minority from the ranks rose higher than captain.

As well as acquiring horses Napoleon also obtained a mistress, the beautiful Pauline Fourès. The wife of a cavalry lieutenant, she had been secretly smuggled aboard one of the transports from France to Egypt. To get her husband out of the way Napoleon sent him on a mission to Malta, but the British captured him and, knowing the romantic situation in Cairo, sent him back to Egypt, where he found his wife installed in Napoleon's oriental palace in Cairo. After he horsewhipped her, Pauline divorced him and continued living so openly with Napoleon that she was nicknamed Cleopatra.

Napoleon showed his knowledge of history by renaming one of his new Arab horses Tamerlan, after the conqueror who had followed the all-powerful Gengis Khan. In 1402 he had invaded Asia Minor and defeated the Ottomans, spreading terror throughout Persia, India and China.

The Arabs bred horses selectively with fanatical attention to purity of line – even though it was dificult to keep males apart from mares who were on heat when there were no fences. The nomadic Bedouins had no written language and memorised the pedigrees and genealogies of their horses. They treated them well, ensuring that agile and fast mares gave birth to foals only from the best stallions. Horse-breeding had become common in Arabia after the time of Muhammad (AD 571–632), but since the area known then as Arabia was about 1,600 miles long and 700 miles wide, differences in climate, soil and nutrition produced several varieties of Arab horse.

Napoleon's innovations, particularly his newly founded Camel Corps in which each camel carried two French soldiers in sky-blue uniforms with white turbans, surprised the Arabs. With speed and precision the French dealt such terrible blows to their enemies from their high perches that even the Bedouin, previously acclaimed masters of the camel, acknowledged their superiority. Seeing his strength and energy, the Egyptians called Napoleon Sultan Kebir, 'the Great Sultan', and paid homage to this little man in the saddle, who could outwit them even in their own deserts.

Napoleon knew that the Turks would retaliate at any moment. Incensed by the invasion, they declared war on France and threatened to invade Egypt. Disturbances followed in Cairo and Turkish troops started to mass in Syria. This threat, combined with lowered French prestige in Europe because of their crushing defeat at the Battle of the Nile, inspired Napoleon with the plan of marching around the

Mediterranean through the Holy Land to attack Constantinople. In February 1799 he set off from Cairo with around 12,000 men, thousands of captured horses and his new Camel Corps.

After a terrible month trekking through the desert, Napoleon stormed the ancient port of Jaffa – despite a heroic struggle on the part of the Turks – and then marched further north, reaching the port of Acre on 17 March. There the Pasha was assisted by Napoleon's old adversary Sidney Smith, by then well and truly involved in the British secret service's undercover plans. Sidney Smith's aide was Phélippeaux, the very man who had sprung him from prison in Paris less than a year earlier and who was now a colonel in the English army. Frustrated by his old classmate, who died of either sunstroke or the plague a few days before the main attack, Napoleon retreated and on 21 May, instead of marching as planned into Europe via Constantinople, started the weary trek back to Cairo in order to arrive before the soaring temperatures of full summer. The camels again showed they were more suited to the desert than horses.

Napoleon's optimism ensured that, failure though the Syrian campaign certainly had been, his entry into Cairo on 14 June through the Gate of Victory was triumphal. Palm branches were strewn in his path and he rode accompanied by beating drums, flying banners and soldiers with palm fronds in their caps. Napoleon's dream of eastern conquest was shattered, but his faith in his cavalry had increased. For, during his campaign and that of his colleague General Louis Charles Desaix, who had just conquered Upper Egypt, the cavalry had again put up magnificent charges.

4

Egypt: Was Marengo Captured Here?

'Bring forth the Horse!' – the horse was brought;
In truth, he was a noble steed . . .
. . . But yet he swerv'd as from a blow;
And, starting to each accent, sprang
As from a sudden trumpet's clang;
Meantime my cords were wet with gore,
Which, oozing through my limbs, ran o'er;
And in my tongue the thirst became
A something firier far than flame.

LORD BYRON,
Mazeppa

Thirteen months after the French army had arrived in Egypt, ten turbulent years after the French Revolution and two weeks before Napoleon's thirtieth birthday, a decisive battle took place at Aboukir Bay, near Alexandria. It was here, according to an exhibit board at the National Army Museum, that Marengo is said to have been captured on a flat spit of land jutting into the sea. The Turks, boosted by their victory at Acre, landed between 12,000 and 18,000 troops. Again they had the support at sea of Sidney Smith in the *Tigre*. This was a vital battle for Napoleon. If he lost, as he had at Acre, the French army in Egypt would be annihilated when the Ottoman Empire retook Alexandria and Cairo.

The Turks fought with ferocity and utter recklessness. On one side lay the open sea, on the other Lake Maadieh and behind the desert. Outnumbered by over two to one, 6,000 Frenchmen faced a formidable army, which was supported by boats at anchor – ready to fire.

Bullets cut down both men and horses. Shot out of their saddles, the men fell like rag dolls. Horses came crashing to the ground breaking the legs, arms and backs of their riders. Riderless horses rolled their bloodshot eyes, searching for help, before they fell on their haunches. Wounded, unable to move, utter despair in their eyes, they raised their heads with a last whinny.

The French, however, were about to achieve a miracle. The battle theories of Napoleon's hero, Alexander the Great, the man who had filled his daydreams since childhood, could now be put into practice by an able pupil. Alexander believed in translating the primitive herd instinct of horses into massive cavalry charges, so that when one horse charged the rest followed.

The cavalry waited, knee to knee, flourishing swords. Murat's order rang out, the trumpet clarion heralded the order: 'Charge!' There was a rush, a sound like thunder, as the men dug in their spurs and swept forward at fantastic speed. Such was their zeal, rhythm and precision that their victory seemed inevitable. Horses, already hit, blood pouring from their bellies, kept galloping, bursting their hearts to keep pace with the horses beside them. The onslaught had a devastating effect on the Mamelukes.

Murat's horses were found galloping everywhere, between the lines, between men, between horses, between life and death, driving the Turks into the water. In vain the Turkish boats offshore sprayed the air with bullets. The men, using the heads of their horses as cover from flying projectiles, lay flat on the animals' necks. The Turks, with their colourful turbans, waving plumes and gaudy banners, swam or drowned in the sea or the lake while attempting to escape or were slaughtered on shore, bleeding into the hot desert sands. Thousands of men and horses perished. Some were rescued by the boats at sea, although the French cavalry hounded the enemy until the sea reached the bellies of their horses. The success of these cavalry charges confirmed Napoleon's belief that horses could make an impact out of proportion to their numbers.

Accompanying Napoleon at the Battle of Aboukir was a superb black Arab horse, covered by a gold-spangled blanket richly embroidered with pearls and other jewels, and his nineteen-year-old groom, a Mameluke slave called Roustam Raza. Both horse and slave had been given to Napoleon as tokens of friendship by a Cairo sheikh. For fifteen years Roustam would follow Napoleon day and night, sleeping on a folding bed at the threshold of his master's room.

Receding with the outgoing tide, brilliantly coloured corpses floated in the very same waters where, eleven months earlier, French ships, sailors and prestige had been sunk by the British. And still the British ships were a threat. Although Napoleon's reputation was boosted by his success at Aboukir, he was fenced in. It was a Pyrrhic victory, won at the expense of freedom. Napoleon, the conqueror of Egypt, could not sail to France – or even safely despatch mail – without risk of immediate death. Forming a near impenetrable barrier around the northern shores, the English ships ensured that the French were hemmed into the country they occupied. The report sent by the British to the Admiralty summed up Napoleon's victory: 'I am sorry to have to acquaint Your Lordships of the entire defeat of the first division of the Ottoman army.'

The British ships were led by the *Bellerophon* – named, ironically, after the Greek hero who caught and rode Pegasus. Little did

47

Napoleon know at that stage that this sturdy ship of the line would be his personal nemesis. Seven years later it would play a major role at the Battle of Trafalgar in the Atlantic, and at the end it would carry him from France in the first stage of his exile to St Helena. Nicknamed 'Billy Ruffian' by her crew, the *Bellerophon* was a ship to fear.

Leading the cavalry was the hot-headed Alexandre Dumas, known as the Black Devil (the father and grandfather, respectively, of the writers of *The Three Musketeers* and *La Dame aux Camélias*). Dumas, the son of a French marquis and his Santo Domingo black slave, was one of Napoleon's most uninhibited critics. Exceptionally strong, tall and handsome with an air of patrician grandeur, he was a striking contrast to Napoleon. Beside him, Napoleon, with his long torso and short legs, looked puny. Dumas's languid, aristocratic confidence made Napoleon's restlessness and adolescent-like nervous energy more obvious. The two men clashed. Napoleon accused Dumas of sedition. Two other cavalry leaders were already Dumas's rivals as brilliant cavalry officers: Napoleon's brother-in-law Victor Leclerc and Murat (soon, also, to become Napoleon's brother-in-law).

Meanwhile Marengo – according to a story often repeated – was captured. This meant that he was pulled from the water, grabbed in the chaos of the bloodied battlefield, or seized from one of the Egyptians. The equine expert Stella Walker, author of dozens of articles and books on horses, wrote:

> to be one of Napoleon's chargers was a dangerous privilege . . .
> The most famous of these chargers was Marengo, a light grey or white Arab stallion imported from Egypt as a six-year-old in 1799 after the Battle of Aboukir . . . The Emperor rode the horse at Marengo . . . he named him after the victorious battle.

He would have been only one of a group of horses, along with about 2,000 prisoners, that were taken. But it is not surprising that there is no record of a horse called Marengo in the French archives of the Egyptian campaign because he would have probably not been called by that name until eleven months later, after the Battle of Marengo, in recognition of exceptional service.

Although it is said that he was captured at Aboukir Bay, Marengo's original name, pedigree and the name of his first owner have been lost. Many horses were taken in Egypt, but few exact details, let alone names, were recorded. The fact that this horse was said to have been six or seven when captured, though, would have been ascertained from his teeth. The incisors of a horse at that age change from an oval shape to being rounded. Recent research from Belgium, however, now maintains that estimating the age of horses by their teeth is not as accurate a method as is generally believed, especially with Arabian horses, because the enamel on their teeth is harder, wears more slowly and shows a different wear pattern from that of other breeds.

Because Marengo was alleged to have been taken during combat against the Turks, he is sometimes called a Barb, rather than a pure Arab. Barbs, which took their name from the Barbary Coast, the area now divided between Morocco, Algeria, Tunisia and Libya, were, as far as Napoleon was concerned, second only to the Arab. 'A good Arab stallion', said Napoleon, 'is the world's best horse. You can with Arab blood get immediate improvements in all breeds . . . The Arabian is a thousand times better than the English Thoroughbred for improving every race, for in him we return to the unmixed purity and power of an original breed.'

The horses of Egypt were smaller than the Thoroughbreds so favoured by Louis XVI and the English. Although from time to time Napoleon rode larger horses, usually to make himself look more impressive, to the amazement and sometimes disdain of his entourage he preferred a small mount. Arabs were the horses on which he was most at ease and his horse-buyers were usually advised not to purchase any large horses for him. Much later, Emmanuel Las Cases described Napoleon's predilection for little horses disparagingly:

> The Emperor was ill-served in saddle-horses but he had eight or ten of them which were acceptable to him: he only wanted to use those. His main officers would have been ashamed to ride them; they were little, skinny and without exterior, but sweet, gentle and reliable; nearly all were entire [non-gelded] and not trimmed [had all their mane and tail].

The victory against the Turks on 25 July at Aboukir Bay not only strengthened the French position in Egypt, but was necessary to Napoleon to wipe out the humiliation of Acre. While news of the victory was rushed to France by couriers taking different routes, Sidney Smith was laying his third trap for Napoleon. Because of the blockade, news from France was scanty. When negotiating for an exchange of prisoners, Smith sent ashore two newspapers, the *Gazette de Francfort* and the *Courier Français de Londres* of 6 and 10 June, in which Napoleon read that the French were discontented with the government at home and that Austria had declared war on Italy and had reclaimed the Italian territory which he taken in 1796 and 1797. Such news, Smith was sure, would lure Napoleon back to France. Once at sea the English would intercept, arrest and imprison him, as Smith himself had been imprisoned in the Temple only eighteen months earlier. And even if he was not caught en route, Smith knew that the French leadership in Paris preferred Napoleon to remain absent because he was far too ambitious and disruptive – his return would pose a threat to them.

Napoleon also had the embarrassment of having his marital situation laughed at on both sides of the Channel. Nelson had earlier captured yet another French ship bearing his official and private letters home. Josephine had resumed her secret romance with the handsome twenty-six-year-old Hippolyte Charles, a young army officer with whom she had first had an affair while Napoleon had been in Italy in 1796. Personal letters, including one to his brother Joseph bemoaning Josephine's behaviour, had already been leaked to the press in London: 'I am undergoing acute domestic distress, for the veil is now entirely rent . . . Make arrangements for a country place to be ready for my arrival, either near Paris or in Burgundy. I expect to shut myself away there for the winter. I am disgusted with human nature. I have need of solitude and isolation.'

5

Napoleon's Return to France

*If thou hast run with the footmen, and
they have wearied thee, then how cans't
thou contend with horses?*

JEREMIAH 12:5

After fourteen months in the East, most of the French troops wished
to go home. Their pay was in arrears. At least 10,000 soldiers had died
of illness or had been killed in battle and the remainder complained of
the heat, the flies, the dread of dysentery or, worse still, the plague.
Other sicknesses had already taken a terrible toll. Lice infestation,
another irritation, caused unbearable itching and acute discomfort
and one in three soldiers suffered from eye disease. The slightest breath
of wind raised clouds of blinding, choking dust. Horses developed
painful and inflamed eyes as well as periodic ophthalmia. The intolerable blaze of the midsummer sun, the burning sand, the lack of
water and shade, all weakened and discouraged men accustomed to a
different climate. Men and horses developed a permanent squint
against the fine flying sand and the ever-glaring sun.

There were some officers, however, who embraced their new life to the full. None took to the ways of the Orient more readily than the aristocratic, pot-bellied, balding and affable Jacques Menou, who, according to his critics, looked more like a bistro proprietor than a general, appearing to be an old man aged more than his fifty years. Arab chroniclers and Napoleon, in his history of the campaign, said he was sixty. Embracing Islam, Menou became a sort of Franco-Arab, donning a turban and attending a mosque during Ramadan, where he repeated prayers like a true Muslim. In March 1799 he was accepted as a convert, married Zobeida, the daughter of a Rosetta bath-keeper, and changed his name to Abdullah Jacques.

Menou's behaviour made him reasonably acceptable to the local population. At some stage he acquired a special horse, a little grey Arab, which he called Ali or Ally after the place where he was captured, Ali Bay. Ali had been mounted by a Dragoon of the 18th Regiment after being taken from the Mamelukes. Forever amiable, Menou gave this horse to Napoleon. It is not recorded where or when this exchange took place, but everything points to it being in Egypt. Apart from it being politic for Menou to make a generous gesture, why he parted with an animal for which he showed affection is puzzling. It may have been because the somewhat corpulent Menou was too heavy for the little Arab, whereas Napoleon at that stage still had the thin, nervous shape of his youth. Ali was an appealing animal and showed patient co-operation when he was being trained. It cannot be stressed too much that Napoleon rode almost frantically and with a disregard for danger. His slapdash riding techniques often came in for criticism.

Ali must have taken to Napoleon, for while Arab stallions are renowned for developing a one-to-one relationship with their masters, they can, sometimes, be evil-tempered and difficult to handle, not only for strangers but for those with whom they are familiar. Napoleon's determination to push on when others would nod off to sleep in the saddle, meant that he required horses which did not tire before he did. As his valet Constant later explained, he had to have only the best horses: 'The Emperor mounted a horse without grace . . . And I believe that he would not have always been very sturdy on the horse if we had not taken so much care to give him only horses perfectly trained.'

When Napoleon felt that he could escape to France quietly without loss of face, the man chosen to hear his secret plans was Menou. As Napoleon did not have authorisation from Paris to depart without his army, he anticipated that even rumours of his proposed exit might be greeted by near mutiny. Elaborate, clandestine plans were made to prepare two remaining frigates, leaving just two ships of the line in Egypt. His return to France, he rationalised, would be advantageous to his stranded troops. Then, and only then, would he be in a position to exert personal influence to send extra ships, supplies and men to destroy the British blockade. Hours before he left, Menou was entrusted with letters informing key people of Napoleon's departure with instructions not to deliver them for twenty-four hours.

Late on the night of 22 August Napoleon and his entourage were rowed away from the shore, leaving their horses loose on the beach. Left saddled and bridled, the animals made their way back to Alexandria by instinct. The sight of riderless horses cantering in from the desert through the city gates raised fears of ambush – until Napoleon's groom was seen leading one of the horses. But had other horses been loaded on to the boats earlier?

So secretive were Napoleon's departure plans that General Kléber received the letter handing command to him only hours after Napoleon had sailed under cover of darkness. The little flotilla was made up of the *Murion*, the *Carrère* and two sloops, which carried, apart from the crew, Napoleon's stepson and aide-de-camp Eugene de Beauharnais, Bourrienne, who was then his secretary, eight officers and scientists, 1,000 sick and wounded soldiers and 200 able soldiers as a special guard.

Knowing the threat the English fleet posed in the waters he was navigating, Napoleon remained in constant readiness to escape, if necessary by going ashore. Once on board he instructed the Admiral of the ship:

Keep close along the coast of the Mediterranean on the African side until you get south of Sardinia. I have a handful of brave fellows and a few pieces of artillery. If the English appear I will run ashore and make my way overland to Oran, Tunis, or some other port from which we may be able to get home.

Considering the size of the vessels, not many horses would have been allocated to the officers, but they would have had at least one each. It is inconceivable, with such escape plans, that horses were not on board. Napoleon's camel, though, was certainly left behind and had to wait for peace to be shipped to France. Strangely enough, the animal that was on that journey – mentioned by Napoleon in conversation later – was a little Egyptian antelope that had so charmed him that he referred to it when speaking at the Institut de France. If Marengo or Ali were on board they would have been forced to endure forty-seven days at sea on dry rations

Hugging the north African coast and moving only at night, their vigilance never ceased. They sailed against such contrary winds and strong coastal currents that the two frigates were blown back towards the port where they had embarked. The English failure to detect them was a puzzle. The young officers – and presumably the animals and men as well – found the tedium of this zigzagging onerous; boredom set in. As for Napoleon, he regaled his friends with ghost stories. However, staying close to the coast was wise because eventually they eluded the British and, near the ancient ruins of Carthage, turned north.

Little did the French realise their luck. Even though the British were doggedly maintaining their blockade in the Mediterranean, their most brilliant commander, Admiral Nelson, who had hunted them down before, was relaxing in Naples, enjoying both adulation as the hero of the Battle of the Nile and a passionate romance with Lady Hamilton.

Although Corsica was not on the itinerary, by chance adverse winds blew the *Murion* to Ajaccio. Even though Corsica is an island where rivalries and feuds last for generations, there was no trouble. Napoleon had, after all, re-established French rule in 1796 and Paoli was once again in England. The only guns that were heard were those fired during a wild boar hunt – a *battue* – when he and his officers went into the forest. The next day he served the game at a grand dinner in his old home.

Casa Bonaparte had undergone a transformation. Gone was the modest apartment Napoleon knew as a child, as were any signs of poverty. The house was no longer shared with relatives. Gone, too, were traces of its occupation by English officers. The affluence accompanying Napoleon's new rank had allowed his mother to refurbish their home and take over the floors the relatives had previously occupied.

As soon as the wind was favourable the two frigates set sail again. Napoleon took a backward glance at the island of his birth, unaware that he would never see it again. Four days later, after narrowly escaping capture by the English fleet, his ships entered the harbour of St Raphaël in the Bay of Fréjus in the south of France. The whole town was in commotion. Even before the anchors were dropped, the harbour filled with boats. Napoleon landed and sped to Paris via Aix and Lyons, leaving men, cargo and livestock to follow. His reputation had been growing with such leaps and bounds that excitement mounted as news of his arrival spread from village to village. In England fury that Napoleon had eluded their blockade was expressed in a caricature in which Nelson was shown caressing Emma Hamilton, while the frigate *Murion* with Napoleon on board passed between the Admiral's open legs.

The prestige Napoleon had acquired as hero of the Italian campaign was untarnished by his failure in Egypt, and his progress to Paris was almost triumphal. The poverty and disorder that he saw confirmed his belief that post-revolutionary France needed change. Inflation, shortages, rationing, conscription, inefficiency and corruption had brought the government to a low ebb indeed. The state was inefficient and nearly bankrupt. The Directoire was detested. Austria again threatened French frontiers. The Royalists were regaining influence. The passions and privations that had caused the Revolution were ready to surface again.

After a stormy reunion with Josephine, Napoleon plotted his *coup d' état*. But he was not seen discussing politics. To disguise his new ambition he frequently attended meetings at the Institut de France although there was no doubt that his interest was genuine. Aware of the importance of the Rosetta Stone and its three inscriptions – hieroglyphic, Coptic and Greek – he made the first speech to the world about its incredible discovery, as well as talking about Egypt's ancient monuments and the link which would be made between East and West if the ruins of the unfinished Ptolemaic Suez canal were excavated to connect the Red Sea and the Mediterranean.

Napoleon's personal horses were kept at rue de la Victoire and at times at Malmaison, the country estate an hour's ride from the centre of Paris which Josephine had acquired in Napoleon's absence. Horses which had lived under the shadows of the pyramids and survived the harsh desert now had to learn to negotiate the cobblestones of Paris and wander in the lush green pastures of the Ile de France.

Some of Napoleon's happiest days in the years that followed were spent at Malmaison, with its spacious grounds and family atmosphere. There he could, for a short time, enjoy riding purely for pleasure and play the role of stepfather to Josephine's two children by her first husband, especially sixteen-year-old Hortense, who was still at Madame Campan's boarding school. 'Nowhere, except on the battlefield, have I seen Bonaparte more happy than in the gardens at Malmaison,' wrote Bourrienne.

On the weekend of 30 October, instead of going to Malmaison, Napoleon visited his brother Joseph at his grand estate, Mortefontaine, west of Paris. His equestrian confidence was given a blow when he took a bad fall. Whether this was because he was riding at breakneck speed or because he simply lost his nerve is not recorded. Nervousness in a rider's hands is felt by the horse and disrupts its steady rhythm. Unlike most of the horses which Napoleon rode, this animal had not been trained for him. He fell against a tree, was knocked unconscious and nearly killed.

Nine days after the accident Napoleon borrowed another frisky grey, taller than his usual mounts, and galloped to the palace of Saint Cloud, which was about a mile from Malmaison. This was the moment for the bloodless *coup d'état* which he had been secretly plotting since his return. The Lower Chamber, in a last spasm of Republicanism, refused to vote. After a tumultuous meeting with the Council of the 'Ancients', followed by another noisy encounter, Napoleon returned to the courtyard. Thinking he was defeated, he called for his horse. The animal was alarmed by the excited roar of over a thousand men all trying to be heard at the same time. As Napoleon tried to mount, it reared, kicked, pawed the ground and bucked. Two grooms steadied the beast with difficulty. Once Napoleon had managed to mount he had problems in keeping his seat and attempted, without success, to ride with style and regain control. To some extent his evident lack of composure in front of the troops and later in the Assembly can be attributed to this contretemps with his horse. In his frustration and humiliation he scratched at his face, causing it to bleed.

The sheer imposing size of the horse gave him some authority as he rode along the ranks shouting: 'Soldiers, can I count on you?', but obviously not enough as most of the men remained silent. Lucien, his brother, then the President of the Five Hundred, demanded a horse and a drum roll and rallied the army. With the attention of the army upon him, his sword against Napoleon's chest, Lucien promised: 'I swear to pierce the breast of my own brother should he interfere with the liberty of the French.' Only then did the troops respond. As he had so often done in the past, Joachim Murat, the ever-dashing and gallant cavalry leader, his jaw badly scarred from a pistol shot at Aboukir, came to Napoleon's aid and entered the Orangerie with his troops behind him, bayonets glittering. With his brother-in-law, Victor Leclerc, beside him, Napoleon rushed into the Council Hall with a column of Grenadiers, crying 'Vive la République!' The sight of the fixed bayonets soon scattered the politicians. In the general mêlée some even climbed out of windows. Finally, the Upper Chamber and a minority of the Lower Chamber agreed to transfer the rule of the largest population in Europe to three consuls: Napoleon, Emmanuel Joseph Sieyès and Pierre Roger Ducos. At two a.m. on 11 November 1799 the three men swore allegiance to the Republic, then made their way to their new official homes in the Luxembourg Palace, the centre of government of the Republic.

Napoleon was gratified by his rise to power, though he was now obliged to spend up to eighteen hours a day confined to an office to show that he was more than just a successful general. He was the driving force which ensured that the Civil Code, known as the *Code Napoléon* – which embodied the legal equality and property rights that had emerged from the Revolution – was completed and a printed copy made available in pocket form with an index. An educational law set up lycées and scholarships.

To relieve the stress of office Napoleon rode for recreation. Later on St Helena he told Las Cases: 'It is necessary for my health for me to ride seven or eight leagues on horseback a day. It is very therapeutic.

Six or seven leagues on horseback per day are a very good way of inducing perspiration.' (A league is equivalent to about three miles.)

Napoleon also frequently visited his new house in the country. His secretary Baron Fain wrote:

The Emperor liked the countryside, and winters at the Tuileries seemed long to him. As soon as he could see from his windows the chestnut trees in the garden sprout their first leaves, he could not wait to have more than one door on the ground floor opened so he could walk out on the lawn and stroll freely down a green path. His impatience was that of a schoolboy. The month of March rarely passed without a trip to Malmaison, at least as long as his marriage to Josephine lasted.

Leading French artists petitioned Napoleon for support for the print industry and he became the first head of state to subsidise this branch of the arts. An abundance of relatively cheap engravings, black and white and also colour, followed – everything from landscape, animals or flowers to portraits and battle scenes. Not only did the arts benefit, but, for the first time, a large part of the population was able to afford reproductions of masterpieces and paintings of the day. By helping the print industry and opening the Louvre, Napoleon widened the audience for art, but he also made himself – and his battles and horses – better known throughout Europe, as well as in every cottage in France. His image benefited as each victory or major happening in his life was reproduced pictorially throughout his dominion.

Within three months Napoleon had changed his residence in the Luxembourg Palace on the Left Bank of the Seine for the Tuileries on the Right Bank. He chose the grand and gloomy royal chambers from which Louis XVI had been forcibly removed seven years earlier. Napoleon had now been promoted to the position of supreme power in France, as First Consul, and a new constitution was drawn up under which he had the power to appoint all public officers and to propose all public measures in peace and war.

His move between the two palaces was accompanied by the sound of trumpets. He sat resplendent in a magnificent gilt state coach drawn by six pale grey horses accoutred with elaborate harness and stiff feathers. Such splendour had not been seen since the heyday of the monarchy. Some said that the First Consul was a man of the Revolution, a Mirabeau on horseback, while others likened him to Frederick the Great – ruler, *philosophe* and leader of armies. Nobody yet accused him openly of using the discarded trappings of royal pomp to glorify himself.

The horses in the procession were a splendid sight. Some were diminutive Arabs, while some were larger, such as those given to Napoleon by Emperor Francis of Austria after his victory at Campo Formio. Behind Napoleon rode another trophy of war symbolising the Orient: the Mameluke Roustam dazzling in his colourful turban, mounted on his prancing Arabian horse, leading the *conseillers d'état*. Brightening up countless dull scenes with his flamboyant silk costumes, he soon became a favourite with journalists and painters.

Post-revolutionary Parisians were ill-prepared to put on displays of grandeur, so most *conseillers* had to travel in rented vehicles with swathes of decoration cleverly hiding their proletarian licence and hiring numbers. Last in the procession was an escort of the cavalry. Splendidly dressed, they were accompanied by a stirring military band. Cheering from the throng was interspersed with shouts of 'Vive la République!' and 'Vive Bonaparte!'

For the review of the troops Napoleon rode an Arab stallion, but which one? Many of his horses were similar in colour and size, and there was often confusion about their identity. Napoleon's personal horses were given high-quality attention by a staff of grooms, farriers, trainers and stablehands. Under Louis XVI the stables had been one of the most extravagant palace departments, where nothing was stinted and overspending was the norm, even though shortly after his accession in May 1774 he abolished *la petite écurie*, reducing the number of his horses from 6,000 to 1,800. Napoleon, by contrast, usually kept around eighty personal saddle-horses, plus pairs and teams of matching carriage-horses, in the Tuileries stables. Preferring everything to run efficiently, he began to introduce a new discipline and stringent economies, including staff reductions.

Unluckily for the little horses from Egypt, there was one employee who preferred the fashionable Thoroughbreds – and whose passion for them led him to become one of the founders of racing in France. Nicolas Rieussel, who had started working in the stables at the age of twelve during the first Italian campaigns, had risen quickly to become provider of fodder to the French army and the consular stables.

Arab horses, with their courage and ability to cover long distances at steady speed, their docility and strength to keep going when fatigued, were sought after for the French light cavalry. Other plusses were their ability to subsist on rough herbage, their hard bones, stamina, beauty, intelligence and sheer personality. But their flat withers and short backs sometimes made fitting them with a saddle a problem. Unlike the Arabs, the English Thoroughbred, bred for speed, excelled in both hunting and racing. Crossed specifically to shine in sporting pursuits, all Thoroughbreds are descended from about a hundred mares and three stallions taken to England in the late seventeenth and early eighteenth centuries: the Godolphin Arabian, or more correctly the Godolphin Barb from Tangier, the Darley Arabian from Aleppo and the Byerley Turk, a Turkish stallion.

Napoleon, recognising horses as a valued part of the army, displayed them prominently and often. As he was very fond of pageants of any kind, the procession to the Tuileries would be the first of many and heralded an era of new stateliness and splendour. The use of stage-managed public spectacle, as well as cavalry, for theatrical effect would often be repeated later.

With his parade, operatic in its grandeur, Napoleon was making up for a decade of dull Republican practices. The generals in showy uniforms of white breeches, jackets edged with gold braid, sported flamboyant tricolour plumes in their bicorn hats. Five years earlier the move to the Luxembourg Palace by the five members of the newly created Directoire had been a reasonably subdued affair in four-wheeled hackney carriages escorted by a small troop of cavalry, their uniforms so shabby that some soldiers had not worn riding boots. Now the horses and men who crossed the river were beautifully decked out. When they passed the Louvre and stopped at the Tuileries, Napoleon, wearing red breeches and jacket, descended from his carriage, mounted his horse and reviewed the Guard. Napoleon's love of spectacle led to other military parades outside the palace becoming one of the major attractions in Paris. At these parades, held every ten days, Napoleon usually rode an Arab. Baron Fain described his preference: 'The horses which the Emperor usually rode were Arabians; of small size, greyish-white coat, good-tempered, gentle gallopers, and easy amblers.'

Despite the evidence in certain paintings, Napoleon's Arab horses were grey: trout grey, slate grey, dark grey, dirty grey, pale grey, blotchy grey, dappled grey, spotted grey, light grey, dark grey with white spots, mouse grey, ash grey, mirror grey, mixed grey, white-grey and clear grey. It is not surprising that the National Archives in Paris confirm that Napoleon's horses were all shades of grey, since in reality white horses are actually grey and turn white only in old age – unless they are albino. Yet white horses helped to shape the Napoleonic myth. Grey horses were painted white in canvases to highlight Napoleon in battle scenes. 'White' horses are usually born chestnut or bay – only the muzzles and eyelids give a clue as to their future colour. By the age of two or three they are usually iron grey. The variable grey of some horses – common among Welsh ponies and Arab horses – is something they are born with; they may eventually turn white, with the mane and legs retaining coloured hairs longer than the coat. In old grey horses which have turned white, pigmented hairs create little spots which are described as 'fleabitten'. The horses often appeared as white in paintings by artists who received Napoleon's support, such as Antoine-Jean Gros and François-Pascal-Simon Gérard, who were both elevated to the status of baron and produced flattering images of their patron and his animals.

A pure white horse, in reality, would have drawn attention to the rider at a distance and made him an easy target. In the British army at this time, when soldiers were told to assemble 'at daybreak' this was defined as 'when you can see a grey horse a mile away'.

Nimble though it is, a small horse can never maintain the high speed over long distances of its longer-legged companions. The incredible velocity of Thoroughbreds is the reason why they became kings of the turf. But the small horse had other advantages: there is less distance between the rider and the ground, for example. And for Napoleon it meant that he did not have to widen his legs too much when astride them – for much of his adult life he suffered pain from urinary and bladder problems. Most of all, though, a general sitting high in the saddle above his troops was an easy target for enemy sharpshooters or artillerymen. Napoleon's caution in riding small horses paid off. In an estimated sixty-six battles only about ten to eighteen horses were killed under him – although this figure is often exaggerated. Apart from their lack of prominence in battle, small horses, especially in military conditions, were also easier to groom, saddle and care for generally – large horses suffered far more from hunger. In bad weather small horses had a better chance of finding shelter on campaign as they could take cover in donkey and mule stables. Most importantly, the smaller the horse, the fewer calories needed. It could keep going longer with smaller rations of grass and oats – especially on marches when fodder was often scarce. But Napoleon also chose Arabs simply because he preferred them.

After his first procession to the Tuileries, Napoleon dictated a press release to *Le Moniteur* for those of his subjects who had not witnessed it. He was one of the first political leaders to be aware of the value of favourable publicity and national events. Ninety-five per cent of France's population of twenty-six million lived on scattered farms and villages, and he realised the importance of getting information to them. At the same time, under his rule freedom of the press was heavily curtailed and censorship was severe.

After installing himself and Josephine in the Tuileries, one of the first things Napoleon did was to move into his rooms busts of the men he admired: Alexander, Brutus, Caesar, Frederick the Great, Washington and Mirabeau – most of whom were famed as fearless riders.

Napoleon, who was always extolling peace but always preparing for war, next set about creating new battalions and squadrons. Although schooled as an artillery man, he relied primarily on flesh and blood – men and horses. The cavalry of the revolutionary armies, which had been in a poor state, was improving, even though enlisting men was often easier than finding enough good horses. After the outbreak of the Revolution in 1789 only sixty-two mounted regiments remained; in 1798 there were eighty-four, and Napoleon added more and also improved standards within them. Less than a month after coming to power, he created a powerful cavalry element for his guard, the Garde des Consuls: a squadron of mounted guides and a 1,018-strong regiment of light horse cavalry, the Grenadiers à Cheval in four squadrons comprising two companies, who were later expanded into the Chasseurs à Cheval. These horsemen were to remain his favourites and he was more often than not seen in their uniform.

Then, as now, efficient communications helped to win wars. Napoleon knew that to control and dominate Europe he needed steady, well-trained steeds for battles and speedy and strong horses for communication. Without the brisk movement of information, weapons and men, he was powerless. Before any campaign, wide networks of spies and cavalry scouts collected precise information – as well as not so precise gossip – on which strategy could be based. On the battlefield, horses were so important that any animal which slipped when carrying an aide-de-camp with a vital message could spell military disaster. To maintain his Empire, Napoleon relied on an efficient diplomatic service, good roads, fast steeds and staging posts with relays of fresh mounts. Since homing pigeons were not widely trusted, the fastest means of communication was by horse; mounted couriers averaged less than a hundred miles a day – seven miles an hour if trotting, ten at a gallop, but it was likely to be less – alternating a steady trot and walking. Travelling had so many hazards that duplicate messages were sent by different routes.

Ali quickly adapted to a range of testing conditions. A few months after a cramped passage to France, surviving on miserable dry rations, he moved into the former royal stables in front of the Hôtel de Longueville opposite the Tuileries. Horses destined for the personal service of the Consul went through a brutal toughening-up process under the riding master, whose aim was to make them reliable and immune to the traumas of battle. Horses had to learn not to react to any sudden noise, let alone the smell of gunpowder and burned flesh. If they could not withstand the shocks associated with battle they were sent away forever, since a frightened horse could cause its rider's death. The hardest lesson that the horses learnt was to stand stock still while gunshot flew close to their eyes, head, legs and body. They were conditioned never to bolt or neigh or stop suddenly unless ordered to do so. Swords were unsheathed close to them and bayonets crossed. Drums were played, pistols and boxes of firecrackers were let off near their ears. Flags were waved in front of their eyes. The riding master drove pigs and dogs between their legs. At other times he threw heavy packages towards the horses. He trained them to respond to commands such as 'A la charge!' 'Au trot!' 'Chargez!' and 'Halte!' In the end they learnt to stay steady under fire. It is said that their training also included being taken at full gallop to the edge of a precipice and then pulled up short, but this may have been an exaggeration.

Napoleon's valet Constant wrote:

It was necessary that, in the midst of the fastest gallop – Napoleon favoured only that kind of pace – the horse was able to come to a dead stop. He needed, in short, only horses which had been tamed and broken. M Jardin, equerry of his Majesty, performed this difficult task with skill and cleverness; and so [Napoleon] was very fond of him . . . He liked good riding masters; so nothing was neglected so that his grooms could receive the best education that could be provided. They were instructed to ride well and with grace and also practised acrobatic skills which would have appeared to only belong to the Cirque Olympique. A Mr Franconi – who at one stage may, like other members of his family, have been a circus owner – was in charge of that part of the education of the pages.

Most horses entering the French army underwent conditioning, as is seen in the 'Instructions for the Manoeuvres of Mounted Troops':

Horses will be habituated to fire by firing pistols at the stable doors when they are being fed their oats. Take care to dwell for a pause between the shots at first, but as the young horses become more accustomed to the fire, repeat the pistol shots more frequently. If among the young horses, there are some who are sufficiently upset to affect the troupe, you must lead them to the stable before beginning the lesson, which should be continued, morning and evening, while they are eating their oats, and to habituate them, separately and little by little, to the noise of firearms. In this way the horses will also become accustomed to the movement and the flapping of the standards and, when in company with the infantry, to the noise of their drums.

Despite training his mounts to withstand the terrible noises and torments of battles, Napoleon appears to have had a certain respect for the animals. When in exile he showed an appreciation of the deeper sentiments of the horse, telling his Irish surgeon, Barry O'Meara, with an irritating lack of humility:

A horse knows his master from the grooms, though the servants [grooms] are more constantly with him. I had a horse myself, who knew me from any other person, and manifested by capering and proudly marching with his head erect, when I was on his back, his knowledge that he bore a person superior to the others by whom he was surrounded. Neither would he allow any other person to mount him, except one groom, who constantly took care of him, and when ridden by him, his motions [movements] were far different, and such as seemed to say that he was conscious he bore an inferior.

Napoleon's personal rule in France ended eight years of turmoil. He set to work making a bridge between the State and the Church; he encouraged French exiles and émigrés to return home; useful public works were commenced; industry and employment were promoted; the government was reorganised. As France started to prosper, luxuries began to reappear, even a new opulent style of furniture.

The Retour d'Egypte Empire-style furniture carried carvings, gilt motifs of crowns, caryatids and griffins. The classical embellishments of Greece and Rome were combined with sphinxes and other symbols of Egyptian antiquity, such as scarabs, the heads and bodies of mummified or stylised Egyptians with bare feet, palm leaves, tripods, rosettes, lotuses and the characteristic sphinx-like, human-headed animal figures. The goddesses and swans of classical mythology mingled with symbols of the Roman warrior – swords, arrows and helmets. Life-like claw feet supported tables, chests and carved stands.

A wave of Egyptomania engulfed the fashionable in Paris. Women were particularly fascinated by the clothes of the Mamelukes, especially the flamboyant silks and bright colours. Pearl grey dresses under 'Mameluke' jackets of taffeta were seen in Paris. While Josephine led the fashion for women, the First Consul's Egyptian horses set a new style in equestrian accessories.

Roustam was acclimatising to France, becoming more than an ordinary *valet de chambre* and bodyguard. Wherever Napoleon went this Mameluke, like a shadow, was to be seen a few yards behind. Sometimes he was on the box of Napoleon's carriage, arms folded, sometimes he was on foot, sometimes on horseback beside the grooms, but he was always there as a reminder of *Egypte française*. Foremost among modern rulers and intellectuals, Napoleon recognised the debt which European civilization owed to Egypt, as was seen by his attempt to bring about a fusion of the secular West with the Islamic East.

With his flowing robes, bright yellow or red turbans and voluminous wide red pantaloons, Roustam became a sign of Napoleon's presence. He was seen galloping at every parade, and as an outrider followed Napoleon on his journeys, carrying his master's field flask, greatcoat, cloak and portmanteau. Baron Fain wrote:

The Mameluke then became a chamber valet on horseback; he could be seen following close to his master, having always at the back of his horse a small case fitted with the spare clothing which could be the most necessary, and keeping in reserve the famous grey frock-coat which the Emperor wore over his clothing in bad weather.

Napoleon's approach to revitalising the cavalry was influenced by the spectacular and wild horsemanship he had seen on the sands of Egypt. Among the elegant new corps he created were one to attract returning émigrés into active service and another to later utilise the abilities of the daring Mamelukes who had moved to France and joined the Consular Guard. With their brilliance and colourful showmanship, they became the flower of the Consular Guard and reinforced Napoleon's romance with ancient Egypt – and his love of dare-devil riding. During parades they did not march but galloped, bringing their horses to an abrupt halt.

Egypt and all things Egyptian remained a feature of Napoleon's life and the influence permeated France. Although Napoleon had lost the opportunity to become an oriental potentate, reminders of Egypt – the Mamelukes, the horses, the antiquities, Empire furniture – formed a fantastic backdrop to his life. As we have seen, the scientific discoveries from his Egyptian campaign were the most enduring results of any of his expeditions. Everything Egyptian was fashionable, just as, half a century earlier, all things Roman had come into vogue after the excavations of Pompeii had begun in 1748.

Napoleon's star might have been rising in Paris, but in Egypt it was falling. His men were still stranded there, hemmed in by the British blockade. The peace talks started early in 1800 between General Desaix and Sidney Smith ended in shambles. Desaix was captured by the British while en route for France and was briefly imprisoned in Leghorn, but after a few months he was released.

6

The Battle of Marengo

Four things greater than all things are –
Women and Horses, and Power and War.

RUDYARD KIPLING,
'Ballad of the King's Jest'

Although succour was sent to the French army marooned in Egypt, little was done to rescue the men. All eyes were on territory closer to home. France was still at war with Austria, and Napoleon, eager to renew the glories of his earlier Italian campaign, raised a new army. He was determined to push the Austrians out of northern Italy, which he had won a few years previously and which had been lost when he was in Egypt. Leaving the core of the new French army on the Rhine, he rapidly assembled a secret force on the shores of Lake Geneva. His plan was for a surprise invasion through Switzerland, which had recently come under French control.

Unpopular though conscription was, most French soldiers were then conscripts. Since its introduction after the Revolution, ways were constantly being devised to escape the call-up. Exemptions were granted for asthma, lameness, imbecility, deafness, lack of teeth, missing fingers, bad eyesight or a missing eye. (Teeth were needed to rip open the cartridges.) A soldier had to be fit enough to withstand long hours of fighting. After a day on the battlefield his shoulder would be black and blue from the recoil of firing anything up to 250 rounds of ball cartridge and his trigger finger would be bruised and swollen. Loading muskets required skill. Such were the problems associated with muskets that some phrases, such as 'to go off half cocked' – where the hammer on the musket is only pulled back halfway and fails to ignite the powder to shoot the projectile – have become incorporated into the English language. Likewise 'He has shot his bolt' refers to a soldier who has forgotten to remove his ramrod from the barrel of the musket and has fired it.

Like a modern Hannibal – minus the elephants – Napoleon led 37,000 troops, 5,000 horses and 58 cannon on a terrifying route over the gigantic, icy mountains. Even though Arab horses are famed for endurance, this daring expedition over the Alps would have been a dreadful ordeal for any horse used to hot, flat desert sands. As for Napoleon, his adaptability and perseverance went without saying; he appeared as much at home in the mists and cold as he had under the blazing sun of the Egyptian deserts. Each man carried weapons, several days' supply of food and bundles of cartridges. Reaching the rugged heights, the slippery, narrow paths could be trodden only in single file. The slightest stumble would, and did, plunge man and beast headlong into the abyss. The mountain pass was so high that, even though spring was a little early, the snow had not yet thawed. Notwithstanding the warm blankets covering them, most Arab horses with their fine coats and thin skin felt the cold terribly. As Arab stallions were too valuable to take risks with – even a cough caused alarm – they received preferential treatment.

This celebrated crossing would later be immortalised in the painting by Jacques Louis David, *Napoleon Crossing the Alps*, in which Napoleon was depicted, according to his wishes, as '*calme sur un cheval fougueux*' – 'calm astride a fiery horse'. David's painting was a glamorised portrait of Napoleon clinging to the horse's mane, with his left foot in the stirrup in an attitude of intrepid daring; the young and handsome leader ignoring deep ravines and nearly perpendicular cliffs as he conquers his fear and the mountains – Napoleon knew well the value of propaganda. In fact, the terrain was so steep and treacherous that for the most hazardous parts he rode a nimble-footed alpine donkey, led by a peasant, while the horses were carefully led through the passes.

The carriages were taken to pieces and each part, including dozens of wheels slung on poles, was borne on the shoulders of two men. The guns were even more difficult to get over the mountains. The barrels of the cannon were dragged in hollowed-out pine logs by a long string of mules in single file. But the poor beasts, pulling such heavy loads, tired before the soldiers, so the men took it in turns to pull their loads.

The challenge for men with horses was enormous. Cautiously, walking sideways with their backs to the cliff-face, watching every movement of their frightened horses, they gently coaxed them along the narrow track. Music reverberated across the valleys. The loud regimental marching songs may have been inappropriate, but the bands played them to boost morale. When an extra burst of energy was needed from the weary soldiers, the tunes of the cavalry charge were beaten on the drums to inspire renewed vigour.

The wonder of this expedition was still with Napoleon years later:

The infantry and cavalry passed one by one, up the path of the mountain, which I had climbed, and where no horse had ever stepped: it was a way known to none but goatherds. Going down the downward slope of the St Bernard Pass was even more difficult for the horses than the ascent had been; there happened, however, but few accidents.

Soldiers, still in single file, placed each foot cautiously as they went down craggy steps of rock and ice, clutching the reins when clouds descended on them, making visibility almost nil. The men ate bread, cheese and wine; the horses were fed with oats, bran and chaff – all of which had to be carried.

At last they arrived at a hamlet at the foot of the Alps. Napoleon had cut off the Austrians' supplies, thus preventing their retreat. A thirty-day campaign followed in which Napoleon seized Milan and Pavia. Among so many military conquests he made a purely personal one, that of twenty-seven-year-old contralto Giuseppina Grassini, the *prima donna* at La Scala, later to be known as *la chanteuse de l'Empereur*. Four years earlier, when he had been madly in love with Josephine and still young enough to equate love with fidelity, he had resisted Giuseppina's advances. This time he asked General Berthier to send for her – and started not only his second well-known adulterous affair, but also her career in France.

The last battle in the campaign, the Battle of Marengo, was fought a mile from the town of Alessandria. Twenty thousand French troops, with about 3,500 horsemen, faced 32,000 Austrians. The disadvantages of fighting on horseback were considerable. If a horse bucked, stampeded and went of control, his rider was next to useless. Once a man in the saddle had pulled the trigger and fired his flintlock pistol, he had only his sword with which to fight. Pistols had to be loaded between shots, and firing and reloading were cumbersome exercises; automatic revolvers and other firearms which could be loaded with magazines of cartridges were yet to be invented. Shooting accurately while charging was also notoriously difficult.

At Marengo, one of the horses which Napoleon rode was an old favourite, Styrie, a grey mare and a veteran of his earlier Italian victories. The first horse entered in Napoleon's register, she had remained in training in France while her master was in Egypt. In the midst of the battle a cannon ball flew between the horse's legs, covering her with earth and taking away a small piece of Napoleon's skin and a piece of his left boot, leaving a scar for life. Horse and rider both narrowly missed being lamed, or worse, and the horse, who had so often narrowly escaped death, was retired after the battle. Other casualties were horrific. The field was so strewn with the bodies of fallen horses and men that when the cavalry galloped the iron shoes of the horses trampled and mangled the faces of the dead.

For nine hours, from eleven in the morning till eight at night, the two armies fought relentlessly. By about midday the French had been driven back two miles and the Austrians thought they had won. At that point Napoleon's old companion from Egypt, General Desaix, galloped across the plains with reinforcements. Armed with sabres, carbines and pistols, the cavalry screened the main army before riding in and pushing the Austrians back. By the end of the day defeat had been turned into brilliant victory, but at great cost. In the midst of the tumult Napoleon heard the words: 'Desaix is dead.' By coincidence, almost at the same hour as Desaix was killed, General Kléber was assassinated by a fanatic while walking on a terrace in Cairo. Napoleon said that the death of of his good friend Desaix was 'the greatest loss he could possibly have sustained'. The same, though, cannot be said of Kléber. Although Napoleon admired his abilities, Kléber often criticised Napoleon and had been furious when Napoleon had given him command of the French forces in Egypt. General Menou, who took over from Kléber, proved himself a more capable administrator than general.

The question as to whether any of the horses obtained in Egypt that later became Napoleon's personal chargers had reached France yet is puzzling. Were they still in Cairo or Alexandria with General Menou? If the horse in the National Army Museum had been at the Battle of Marengo, he must to have come back with Napoleon on the *Murion*. Any horse that returned with Desaix would not have had time to be trained to carry the most important man in France into battle. As so many thousands of lives depended on Napoleon, whatever, horse he rode had to be hardened to survive the noise and shocks of the battlefield. A few French writers, including the esteemed Louis Merllié in an article, 'Le cavalier Napoleon et ses chevaux', published in 1980, and Jacques Branet, say that that Desiré and Ali were also present at Marengo. Desiré, a stallion (not to be confused with the mare Désirée who was at Waterloo), had come from the royal stables at Versailles, but Ali definitely came from Egypt, so he must have been given by Menou to Napoleon earlier in Alexandria or Cairo and returned on the *Murion*. But there is no mention of the horse who was depicted in James Ward's romantic lithograph as Marengo. This battle has always been presented in England as the one in which Marengo made his debut on the battlefield with Napoleon, the start of his fifteen years as part of a mighty fighting force. As a result of Ward's emotional treatment, Marengo would be remembered as the horse who had feelings for his master. Indeed, he was sometimes spoken of with the kind of veneration accorded to Bucephalus, the stallion favoured by Alexander the Great.

According to the old RUSI Museum catalogue, Marengo 'was ridden by him [Napoleon] at the Battle of Marengo, and named after the victory'. The name, though, appears nowhere else, but then the names of Napoleon's horses disappear, reappear and change over the years. It is possible that 'Marengo' may have been a nickname – Napoleon had a predilection for renaming those close to him, both horses and women. (As noted earlier, his first wife Rose became Josephine. One of his mistresses, Pauline Fourès, was called Bellilote while another, Josephine Weimer, who was known on the stage as Mademoiselle Marguerite Georges, was renamed Georgina.) Spontaneous endearing names, too, were later bestowed on horses; Intendant became Coco; Cirus was rewarded for his courage with the nickname of Austerlitz; Cordoue became Cuchillero; Bonaparte became Numide; Moscou was nicknamed Tcherkès. The pet name for Ingénu is supposed to have been Wagram after the battle. Marie was otherwise known as Zina. Some of these names were used very casually; for example, nowhere in Napoleonic bureaucracy was Cirus referred to as Austerlitz. Some of them took over from the original names, some were noted in both registers, but others were used informally. The two registers, *Le Registre d'Ordre du Grand Ecuyer* and *Le Registre du Contrôle de l'Equipage de Selle*, kept at the National Archives, help us to identify Napoleon's horses, known as 'the horses of His Majesty's rank'.

At Marengo, twelve hours of battle had left more than 20,000 men, dying and dead. Nobody, of course, counted the crippled and dead horses. Their legs torn from their bodies, they screamed, struggled and died in convulsive agony. Those still with legs kicked in pain. Their whinnying echoed through the night, blending with the groans and screams of the men. As always, the stench of corpses accompanied victory – horses take longer to bury than men. Ravens and crows soon started their clean-up work, picking out the tenderest flesh first.

There was a small number of vets to help the animals. The profession was still in its infancy, even though the first veterinary school in the world had been founded over thirty years earlier, in Lyons, in 1762. Each regiment received at least one graduate from the much improved veterinary college. Horses were submitted to bleeding, physicking and blistering, administered by unskilled men with old-fashioned, insanitary instruments. They extracted fragments of shot and steel. Wounds were drained and arsenic was given in small doses for various ailments.

An army of horses had to be supported by a large number of farriers, vets and grooms. Lameness and sore backs alone put huge numbers out of action. The well-worn adage still held true: no foot, no horse. Badly-fitting saddles caused skin to rupture and bleed. Many troopers were casual about grooming and feeding their horses, let alone attending to their ailments, so sores and ulcers on backs caused an alarming wastage of animals.

The day after the battle, the Austrians sent the flag of truce to Napoleon. He signed a treaty with them which gave northern Italy back to France. In five weeks he had crossed the Alps and regained Italy.

Beside the bivouac fires outside his tent Napoleon was dictated victory notices for Paris, while a scouting party scoured the country-side for food. They found a couple of chickens, a handful of onions, some white wine and olive oil. In a ruined and looted garden there were bay, thyme and parsley . . . Chicken Marengo was born, a recipe, like almost everything Napoleonic, with a thousand variations. As so often, the troops were expected to find their own food, a continuation of revolutionary policy that armies should be self-sufficient and live off the land. This policy, though, was not as extreme as it sounds, as men were often issued with biscuit and other basic rations.

Hard as it was to extract food from the local inhabitants, it was harder still to find provisions for the horses. Yet the speed and mobility of the army was dependent on their health. Unfortunately, the proper food for horses was not always available so getting fodder and water to animals on campaign was an enormous task. Maintaining the supply of tons of fodder, as well as gallons of water, needed daily by thousands of horses when marching, was always a major challenge. As most European cavalry horses stabled at home bases were fed on high protein diets of oats and hay, the sudden change to local grasses when on campaign could cause immense suffering. If horses were fed a lot of hard food, such as oats, and then not worked enough, they got a kind of cramp in their loins (azoturia). But if, working hard and being well fed, they were then suddenly given just grass or hay, they lost condition and would not have enough energy for a day of battle or marching. Unknown grasses could be poisonous, so horses could not graze in any new field, and a perpetual problem was the resentment of local farmers and peasants faced with the arrival of an army of hungry men and horses.

The victory cemented Napoleon's position as ruler of France. The Battle of Marengo was the turning point, the beginning of Napoleon's rise to power and a period of consolidation for him. The very word 'Marengo' became synonymous with luck. He was always inclined to favour soldiers who had been with him at the battle and his career, in his own mind, was separated into pre-Marengo and post-Marengo years. The electrifying impact of the victory was seen everywhere. When messengers arrived to announce it in Paris, workers rushed into the streets avid for the news of the battle. Cafés were full late into the night and toasts were drunk: 'Vive la République!' 'Vive le Premier Consul!' For a few hours France stood still while millions celebrated. Guns thundered, bonfires were lit and victory posters spread the news.

Napoleon, leaving Milan on 25 June, reached Lyons three days later and then passed through Dijon. Paris, decked with flags and ablaze with lights, greeted the victor on 3 July. After the boom of cannon and the bells of Notre Dame announced his arrival, people flocked to the Tuileries to see their hero, who made appearances on the balcony. Later he enjoyed a few days of rest at Malmaison, indulging in his almost English passion for fresh air and exercise, often asking for windows to be opened while everyone else froze. Open air was, he said, conducive to 'the expansion of ideas'. Sometimes, to the horror of the older government men, Napoleon worked on the ground without chairs or table. The statesman Charles Maurice de Talleyrand, Foreign Minister under both Barras and Napoleon, complained:

I arrived at Malmaison . . . where I found the First Consul had established his office on one of the bowling greens. Everyone was sitting on the grass which Napoleon did not mind in the least as he was wearing leather boots and kid breeches – and he is used to camping. But as for me in silk breeches and silk stockings – can you imagine me sitting on the lawn! I am full of rheumatism! What a man! It was as if he was in a camp!

A month after Napoleon's return from Italy, an immense crowd followed him during the celebrations for the anniversary of the storming of the Bastille. People seemed more interested in Napoleon than the ceremony. Members of the government marched from the Tuileries across the river, passed Les Invalides and on to the Champ de Mars to present the colours captured in Germany and Italy. Frenzied old men, women and children dashed near the legs of the horse Napoleon was riding to get near him, touching the gilding on the saddle and kissing the hem of his uniform.

Napoleon's new battalions were led by officers very different from those seen in the years when France was ruled by the Bourbons. In the Republican army promotion was not dependent upon family connections and more than half the captains were promoted from the ranks. The meteoric rise of humble corporals was the result not only of egalitarian ideas and reaction against the archaic traditions of the Bourbons, but of the lack of able candidates after the Revolution. Before the Revolution, officers were recruited from the aristocracy and the landed gentry and as late as 1780 the dominant position of the aristocracy in the army was being strengthened. A decree from the Minister of War forbade the promotion of commoners to higher ranks in the army and limited the minor nobility to inferior positions. Reversing this decree after the Revolution was not difficult, but finding good horses with pedigrees after the aristocracy's departure was a severe problem. As land-owning nobles had been the force behind both horse-breeding and the military, their flight left an enormous shortage of educated men able to command, as well as a dearth of swift, well-trained horses. Some of the men who were promoted, although quick and brave, had had no education or instruction at a military academy. Out of the twenty-six marshals later created by Napoleon, only nine had been officers before the fall of the monarchy. Just three, Davout, Marmont and Grouchy belonged to the old *noblesse* of France. The need for officer material paralleled the need for good horse stock.

Back from the battlefield Napoleon was in his office at the Tuileries. He introduced a new tax system, which was coupled with the foundation of the Bank of France. Paris again rang with church bells and, as in the old days, the Angelus summoned people to prayer. After a decade of silence, on Easter Day 1802 religious ceremonies were conducted in Notre Dame by bishops who were paid by the state. Although the Roman Catholic establishment had been destroyed, as had its independence and its wealth, the Church was allowed to function again. And science was given a platform.

Napoleon's interest in science turned him into the first European ruler to give scientists a place of honour in the state. He had been elected to the Mathematical and Physical Class of the Institut National, at the age of twenty-eight. He gave government portfolios to scientists and later elevated six of them, including Georges Cuvier, known as the father of comparative anatomy and palaeontology, to his newly created peerage. Strangely, although some of Napoleon's scientists created colossal gunpowder factories, Napoleon did not harness technology to improve existing weapons. His troops continued to use rifles, bayonets, muskets, cannon and other equipment – all slow and cumbersome to load – similar to those that he had trained with as an artillery cadet under the Royalists. He concentrated his genius on tactics, strategy, artillery and horses.

War was never far away. Across the Channel the English were plotting the restoration of the Bourbons. Two years after the execution of Louis XVI, the Dauphin was declared dead and Louis' obese younger brother in exile assumed the title of Louis XVIII. He was one of about 25,000 homeless aristocratic émigrés and clergy who had sought refuge in Britain. Britain was not only an overt threat to France, it also welcomed the Royalist underground, who were scheming to regain the French throne. The only surprise about the departure of British troops for Egypt to rout the French was that they had not been sent earlier.

In Paris the police uncovered subversive plots hatched in Britain. Vigilance against the threat of assassination was non-stop. On Christmas Eve a dramatic attempt on Napoleon's life caused the death of ten people and left twenty-eight wounded and forty-six houses badly damaged. Between the Tuileries and the theatre, where Napoleon was on his way to see a performance of Haydn's Creation, there was a terrible explosion – a cart carrying a bomb blew up. By luck the splintering glass, falling stones and collapsing houses missed Napoleon. The nearby Opéra was rocked by the explosion, but the musicians carried on playing. When Napoleon arrived in his box, a little late but as if nothing had happened, the audience gave him a standing ovation. Although the black horse pulling the cart with the bomb was killed by the explosion, his horseshoes, a macabre clue, led the police to his master's arrest – and to a plot masterminded by the secret service in England. Recent research has revealed that Sidney Smith was involved.

War or peace, France continued conscription, troops were trained, battles were fought overseas and the whole of Europe was scoured for horses. So severe was the equine shortage that for years, even though France was Europe's richest agricultural country, no horses, only mules, were exported.

Contrary to Napoleon's original plan, the invasion of Egypt resulted in only a small number of Egyptian horses returning to France to augment French stock. Napoleon never relaxed his drive to capture and requisition horses, or the huge training programmes for both horses and men, and selective horse-breeding schemes. The brick building which housed the Riding School in the garden at Fontainebleau stands today as a reminder of his fanatical determination to improve equestrian standards. Years later on St Helena he told Las Cases how he had introduced grooming for horses at the military schools he had set up. Las Cases wrote in his memoirs:

> that nothing was more useful [than grooming]; that he had given particular orders for it in the military school at Saint-Germain. I was vexed that such an idea had escaped me; I seized it eagerly, and my son still more so . . . The Emperor, whom I informed of it, seemed pleased, and condescended to make him go through a sort of little examination. Our ride lasted nearly two hours and a half.

Napoleon studied every aspect of stable management, from diet to breeding, from horseshoeing to veterinary care. With diet, though, his methods were sometimes too stringent. Once when driving from Paris to Ruelle, a town well known for its cannon foundries, he complained of the length of the journey and asked what would shorten it. 'More oats!' was the reply. Differences of opinion existed then, as now, about the effects of diet, especially oats, on performance. Napoleon's belief that oats speeded up the horse, but that too many without enough activity led to health problems, was unusual then, but accepted today. Oats were then believed to be a superior all-round food for horses.

7

The French Army Returns
from Egypt

Look, when a painter would surpass the life,
In limning out a well-proportion'd steed,
His art with nature's workmanship at strife,
As if the dead the living should exceed;
So did this horse excel a common one,
In shape, in courage, colour, pace and bone.

WILLIAM SHAKESPEARE,
Venus and Adonis

For four-and-a-half-years French guns across Europe were all but silent. The period between the Battle of Marengo in 1800 and the Battle of Austerlitz at the end of 1805 was the longest interval in the Napoleonic era without French guns firing on battlefields on the continent. Most European countries were intimidated by Napoleon's powerful position – all but England.

In March 1801 Sir Ralph Abercromby, a Scottish general, led a successful amphibious assault across the Mediterranean on entrenched

French positions in Egypt. His Anglo-Turkish force of 18,000 included the Black Watch in kilts. The instant they were ashore they were faced with a fierce charge by the French cavalry, whom they decimated with volleys of musketry. Soon the devastating, but not unexpected, news arrived in France that the French forces had lost Cairo and the whole of Egypt to the British. Napoleon took it out on his horse. General Rapp, one of Napoleon's aides, later reported to Napoleon's friend General Junot:

> As long as we were in view of the castle, the general walked his horse, but once we reached and passed the gate he pushed his horse, dug spurs into his belly and the poor beast climbed at full hunting gallop, up this stoney road, to Bougival . . . I who have seen him, I know it is not just bad humour he has, it is grief, it is sorrow.

For Napoleon, horse-riding was a panacea. He rode when he was unhappy, when sick, when stressed – or just for relaxation. Once, complaining of a persistent headache, he said: 'For it to get better it would be necessary for me to gallop for three or four hours.'

Within a few months of Abercromby's assault, the British started transporting the French soldiers and baggage – their weapons, equipment and whatever possessions they could carry – back to France. On 31 July and 7 August French soldiers, Mamelukes in their colourful costumes, as well as some horses, were loaded on eighteen English ships at Rosetta. In October, when the last French soldier had left Egyptian soil, Menou returned to France with his Egyptian wife, Zobeida, their child and a few horses.

The evacuation of Egypt led to peace between France and Britain, the Peace of Amiens, 1803–4. With the truce, Irish and English horses could, at last, be imported into France officially and the English could flock to the continent. Shut out of Europe by ten years of hostilities,

85

visitors now made up for their missed Grand Tours, little realising that these thirteen months would be their last chance to see Paris until 1814. Eighty-one British Members of Parliament, sixty-one peers and thirty-three peeresses, some accompanied by their children, not to mention less exalted citizens, came to France during the peace. Visitors were delighted to find that the gaiety, splendour and sense of style so characteristic of Paris had survived the Revolution. Visiting the Louvre was *de rigueur*, as were the new eating places called 'restaurants'. While Versailles had been the creation of the Bourbons, Paris was to be the glory of Napoleon – he was making it into 'the capital of the civilised world'.

All visitors wanted a glimpse of the First Consul. One popular place for viewing was outside the Tuileries on Sundays, where they could see Napoleon astride one of his light grey Arabian horses as he reviewed his Garde des Consuls – the best troops and cavalry in France. In October 1802 a squadron of 172 Mamelouks de la Garde from Egypt was added to this personal guard. The review was no mere ceremony, but a serious inspection in which questions were asked and answered and noted by the accompanying Chief of Staff in a green pocketbook. Napoleon was usually seen in his unbuttoned *redingote grise*, under which he wore the green uniform, piped with scarlet of the mounted Chasseur of the Guard, a white vest, white breeches and soft riding boots. His plain costume contrasted with the more impressive trappings of his horse. The saddle-cloth and holster-cap were edged with a rich fringe and the stirrups, as well as the bit and bridle buckles, were gold-plated. The reviews, too, had unexpected touches of splendour. Napoleon adopted and adapted the Egyptian jewelled saddle-cloths and finely plaited harnesses. Saddles, harnesses and bridles which were previously utilitarian had become more glittering and ornate. The leather for bridles was rolled, and often braided or laced with gold. One visitor who was impressed by Napoleon's horsemanship was the writer Fanny

Burney, who had married a French émigré, Alexandre d'Arblay:

> Bonaparte, mounting a beautiful and spirited white horse, closely
> encircled by his glittering aides-de-camp, and accompanied by
> his generals, rode round the ranks, holding his bridle indifferently
> in either hand, and seeming utterly careless of the prancing,
> rearing, or other freaks of his horse, insomuch as to strike some
> who were near me with a notion of his being a bad horseman . . .
> he only appeared to me a man who knew so well he could
> manage the animal when he pleased, that he did not deem it
> worth his while to keep constantly in order what he knew, if
> urged or provoked, he could subdue in a moment.

Another English visitor, Delabere Blaine, noted the preferential treatment given to a horse said to be Napoleon's favourite stallion, which
was taken from the Tuileries stables to the quieter and greener Jardin
des Plantes, the former Jardin du Roi, which was both a botanic garden
and zoo, near the university on the Left Bank of the Seine. Blaine later
wrote in his *Encyclopaedia of Rural Sports* (1840) in the section on Arab
horses: 'the celebrated white Arabian stallion, of which Buonaparte was
so fond, that it was usually kept in the Jardin des Plantes, on which spot
the author took the portrait represented by fig. 144 [see page 83]. This
horse, it is evident, was small.' An intriguing point in the account is that
it establishes that even as early as 1802 a single horse was distinguished
as Napoleon's special horse. (Although this horse is likely to have been
Ali, it could equally well have been Marengo, later exhibited in London
and advertised as Napoleon's favourite charger.) In the sketch the
initials 'NB' are branded on the right flank of the horse. It is difficult to
see how the hair would have later grown over the 'B' of such a prominent
mark and could have been changed later to the more elegant imperial
'N' when Napoleon became emperor.

Later in the century Major-General W. Tweedie, in his book *The*

*Bonaparte's charger kept at the Jardin des Plantes in Paris,
thought to be Ali. This illustration appeared in an encyclopaedia
published in June 1840.*

Arabian Horse, referred to the horse kept at the Jardin des Plantes:

> It is pretty certain that Napoleon brought over from Egypt, in
> 1799, after the battle of Abû-Kîr [sic], a light-grey barb, which
> he rode at Marengo. Either this animal, or another of the same
> colour called A'lî [sic], taken at the battle of the Pyramids, in
> Egypt, in 1798, may have been the 'small horse' which Delabere
> Blaine, whose working period was in the first half of our century,
> delineated in his *Rural Sports* with the explanation that he saw it
> in the Jardin des Plantes, where, owing to Bonaparte being 'so
> fond of it,' they usually kept it.

The horse at the Jardin des Plantes must have been the same one
which Napoleon's valet, Constant, later wrote about in his memoirs:

> The Emperor took to those horses which were very beautiful . . .
> He had an Arab horse of rare instinct of which he was very fond.
> All the while he was waiting for his rider he did not seem at all
> graceful and he was difficult, but the moment he heard the
> drums beat to announce the Emperor's coming he drew himself

up proudly, shook his mane and pawed the ground with his foot, and so long as the Emperor was in the saddle he looked the most beautiful horse that anyone could hope to see

This 'impossible to ride until . . .' or 'possible to ride only by . . .' is the conceit of the horseman – and is found right through history. Alexander the Great and Julius Caesar both had horses which it was said nobody else could ride.

Whether Delabere Blaine was one of the scores of visitors presented to Josephine and Napoleon and later invited to the large and lavish monthly dinners at the Tuileries is not recorded. At one such dinner the ingenious English artist Thomas Phillips, dressed as a waiter, stood under the columns sketching Napoleon's face on the white cuffs of his shirt. Refusing to sit for a portrait, Napoleon instead gave Phillips permission to attend a court function as an onlooker. The Duke of Northumberland, a military man, had not made the trip to Paris, but commissioned Phillips (later known for his canvas of Byron in Greek national costume) to paint the First Consul. Among those received by Napoleon were Lord Holland and his celebrated and beautiful wife Elizabeth, who turned Holland House in London into a meeting place for politicians and leaders of society. Lady Holland would later be influential in promoting the Napoleonic legend. Another visitor to Paris was Sir Charles Blagden, later Secretary to the Royal Society in London, who wrote to its president Sir Joseph Banks, the English botanist who had sailed around the world with Captain Cook:

I have observed likewise that the First Consul is fond of animals, both from what he said respecting the Ornithorhynchus [the platypus which Banks had presented to the museum] and from the manner in which he spoke at the meeting of the Institute last month, respecting an antelope he brought from Egypt, and of which he appeared to be really fond . . . The most acceptable present which could be made to the First Consul, would be a pair of live kangaroos . . . the gentlemen of the Jardin des Plantes have been endeavouring to negotiate an exchange with the dealers in animals in London, proposing to give one of their lions for one or two kangaroos . . . The park at Saint Cloud where he is going to reside, would be an excellent place for a little paddock of kangaroos.

Blagden made a plea for the Rosetta Stone to be returned to the French. It had been housed at the British Museum since 1802 and has since become one of the museum's best-known exhibits. His request was ignored, as was his letter of 25 May 1802, which recommended Napoleon be made a Fellow of the Royal Society.

Napoleon's interest in animals impressed another visitor to the Tuileries, the former Lord Chancellor, Lord Erskine, who had attempted to get a bill through Parliament to prevent cruelty to animals. On his return he told the *Morning Chronicle* that he had spoken to Napoleon about suppressing bull-baiting, and he had replied: 'Of all my brave fellows at the Bridge of Lodi or the Plain of Marengo, how many ever saw a bull-baiting or a boxing match?' A few years later Napoleon introduced a practice which benefited animals all over the world. He built the first abattoirs on the outskirts of Paris and pioneered a ban on the slaughtering of animals in individual butchers' shops in the city – a source of cruelty, filth and pestilence.

The English craze for things French balanced the earlier French craze for things English. Despite being frowned upon by the First Consul, no official action could stem this fashion. The teaching of the English language in French schools was discouraged – although French was still part of the curriculum in most English schools. In France men preferred to shave with English razors and longed to know about the exclusivity of English men's clubs such as White's and Boodle's. People wanted to wash with English soap from Bromley and Windsor, drink English tea (but without the milk), eat *rosbif à l'anglais* (but not English nursery-type puddings), ape English manners, wear frock coats and riding coats (which became *les redingotes*), have dresses made from the new English fabric – a fine transparent muslin called cambric – and learn to play whist. They also wanted to look at sporting prints and caricatures modelled on those of England, and sit in English-style mahogany chairs with open backs. The most daring, like Napoleon's wife Josephine, were making romantic English gardens – although Napoleon preferred formal French gardens. Even though England had been France's enemy for years, the Luxembourg Garden reflected horticultural anglomania which had first become fashionable in France at the end of Louis XV's reign. The fashion for things English could be seen in chateaux and large houses, many of which copied the English idea of a fine lawn in front of the stables. Napoleon's preference for riding little Arabs was almost a stand against anglomania; on the eve of the Revolution most of the King's personal horses at Versailles had been English Thoroughbreds which were still much sought-after as saddle-horses.

Anglomania extended to horse-racing. England, the country where organised racing, 'betting on the races' and attending the annual bloodstock sales originated, still led the way in breeding horses for competition rather than military use. Race-goers vied with each other to get copies of the *Racing Calendar* and the *English Stud Book* or hear the latest from the Jockey Club, which had been founded in 1752. English racing had an aristocratic cachet unknown in post-revolutionary France despite the tremendous interest in the sport. In 1805 Napoleon issued a decree which established horseracing under the control of the Ministry of the Interior: 'Horse races shall be established successively in the departments of the Empire most

91

notable for the quality of horses which are bred there. Prizes shall be awarded to the swiftest animals.'

During the Peace of Amiens an almost Bourbon-like etiquette started to take over from the gay, carefree informality of the consular days at Malmaison. Dinner alfresco under the trees, was no more. Aware of his growing prestige, Napoleon abandoned Malmaison as his official summer residence in favour of the nearby palace of Saint Cloud, which was impressive and could accommodate more guests and staff. One of the first innovations at Saint Cloud was a stud farm, from which some distinguished chargers emerged, including Coquet, Turcoman, Courtois, Emir and forty-odd others.

On Napoleon's thirty-third birthday in 1802 a 300-piece orchestra gave a concert at the Tuileries to celebrate the announcement by the Senate that he was now Consul for life, despite the efforts of a growing number of intellectuals to limit his increasing ambition. Amidst other festivities was a Te Deum in the cathedral of Notre Dame, where an amazing thirty-foot star made of lamps sparkled above the cathedral's tower. At this time Camille Jordan's critical pamphlet *Meaning of the National Vote on the Question of the Consulship for Life* was seized before sale and the author narrowly escaped arrest.

Napoleon was given the power to name his successor. Eyes turned to Josephine, then nearly forty, to produce an heir. After six years of matrimony she was still barren, even though she had had two children during her first marriage. To save her position she hinted that Napoleon was infertile – although she feared that a pregnancy of one of his mistresses would prove his ability to father a child. Napoleon was encouraged to divorce – for the sake of the succession – by his brothers and sisters, who loathed Josephine.

Every near-fatality, every daring ride over rough country high-lighted the void that would follow Napoleon's death. On one occasion in 1803 he was knocked temporarily unconscious after taking the reins of a four-horse carriage while he and Josephine were driving in the grounds at Saint Cloud. The four horses bolted before Napoleon had time to regain control and crashed the carriage against a railing. He was hurled to the ground from the height of the coachman's seat. This accident, according to some medical experts, had a devastating effect on his future life. Dr Milo Keynes, the great-grandson of Charles Darwin, writing in the *Journal of Medical Biography* (1996), insists that Napoleon's loss of flair, increasing slowness and weight gain were a result of this accident: 'This was the beginning of Fröhlich's disease, the premature failure of the pituitary gland.' He goes on:

> Hypopituitarism usually results from a pituitary tumour pressing on surrounding structures, giving headaches and underproduction of the hormones produced in the rest of the gland; it may also result from disease of the hypothalamus. Napoleon did not have headaches, or show any evidence of oversecretion of hormones from a pituitary tumour, and this encourages the idea, not previously made, that his hypopituitarism was due to damage to the blood supply of the pituitary, even though this is rare.

Increasing obesity with associated somnolence, along with a lowering of the output of the male hormone testosterone, causing loss of body hair, and lack of libido, are among the results of this disease. Dr Keynes added that it was only later, around 1812, that the symptoms of pituitary dysfunction were fully evident.

The End of Peace

Travellers to France were aware that both Napoleon and George III had reasons to end the peace at any time and that smuggling, which had thrived when the coasts were blockaded, would soon be resumed. Clauses in the Treaty of Amiens stipulated that England was to relinquish Malta while France was to quit southern Italy. Each country waited for the other to act first, but there was a stalemate. Napoleon's policy in Italy irritated the British and, as Napoleon continued to ignore their protests, they declared war. On 16 May 1803 *The Times* announced that George III had recalled his Ambassador from Paris and that the British government had authorised the seizure of French shipping. Napoleon responded violently. He would make war on the trade which was Britain's strength. While the English fleet scoured the seas, paralysing French commerce, the French ensured that every continental market was closed to British goods. No produce coming, directly or indirectly, from Britain or British colonies would be admitted to French ports. He gave immediate instructions to arrest any Englishmen under the age of sixty in France as prisoners of war. Among the 700 detained for between seven and ten years was the son of Sir Ralph Abercromby, who a few years earlier had driven the French out of Egypt.

During the summer of 1803, while French troops were amassing along the Channel and North Sea coasts ready for a second Norman Conquest of Britain, hundreds of flat-bottomed invasion barges were built to transport French troops and weapons. Napoleon would become the 'master of London, Parliament and the Bank of England'. A huge flotilla was assembled in the harbours of Etaples, Boulogne, Ambleteuse, Calais and as far away as Flushing. Today the Colonne de la Grande Armée in Boulogne overlooks the site from where Napoleon surveyed his main army camps and from where, through his giant telescope, he gazed at the walls of Dover Castle. For two years the English lived in almost daily expectation of the arrival of the French, while the mighty army of 176,000 men were turned into such bronzed, muscular, well-fed soldiers that Napoleon could boast: 'Surely there is no finer army in Europe than mine today?' Although readying for a naval exercise, horses were not forgotten. Special stables were made in the barges and ashore the cavalry was being trained to the peak of perfection.

With his keen sense of history, Napoleon must have known of the tragic deaths of the two men who had led invasions into England: both William the Conqueror and William of Orange died after falling from horses. Twenty-one years after the invasion of 1066, William the Conqueror died after his horse stumbled as he rode through the burning town of Mantes and he was thrown to the ground. William III died in 1702, fourteen years after he had landed at Torbay to take over the throne. His death was caused when his horse stumbled over a molehill.

Napoleon, too, was not without his falls. He was nearly thrown when his horse stumbled on a wooden peg among the cobbles of a street in Boulogne. Another time on the coast he had to stop his mount dead so as not to trample a child who had rushed in front of him. He fell over the horse's neck and, picking himself up, muttered: '*Sacré mioche!*' ('Bloody kid!'). Similarly, he later toppled over a woman in Germany. After stopping to see that she was not badly hurt, he arranged for money to be given to her. The intensive training that every horse ridden by Napoleon had to go through meant that neither person was injured. That training was well tested when he was riding along the narrow path above the headlands along the Boulogne–Calais coast, where cliffs drop precipitously to the sea and make for treacherous riding. During his innumerable visits, Napoleon was often seen taking a long, fast recreational ride before six a.m. along the cliffs or over the sandhills. Because he 'skated' in the saddle, his riding breeches were frequently sent to Paris to be patched and darned. His endurance on horseback is illustrated by the ride he made one day in order to reach Calais quickly. He had to cover a distance of forty kilometres. Riding a grey horse, he did not dismount – except for a short halt at Ambleteuse – until he reached his destination.

Napoleon promoted every aspect of travel. Distances shrank as more carefully bred horses became available and roads were improved. He encouraged the development of fashionable lighter, faster coaches with springs and lamps, pulled by lighter and faster horses.

Napoleon's so-called 'Army of England' was ready to be shipped at a moment's notice across the Channel – once he had command of the Channel for three or four days. He had no fixed landing place in mind, but preferred the coast of Kent, near Chatham, from where he planned to make a rapid march on London. Warlike preparations went on apace on both sides of the Channel. The nursery rhyme about 'ten thousand men . . . he marched them up to the top of the hill, and he marched them down again' was a popular jibe at the military incompetence of George III's second son, Frederick, the 'Grand Old Duke of York', who was in charge of the British army and ready to face Napoleon. The Duke, who was so large that he dwarfed his horse, had to support his enormous girth on legs which appeared too weak for the task.

To defend themselves in the approaching conflict the English dotted the south coast with seventy-four circular Martello towers, each with walls nine feet deep and armed with swivel guns and howitzers. Such fear of invasion had not been felt in England since the Spanish Armada and each able-bodied man was ready to fight. By 1803 the Loyal Volunteer militia service, which had first assembled in 1797, numbered about 460,000 men.

While the army were camped on the coast, military operations and training continued throughout France. Napoleon's methods of training horses in his stables spread to newly opened riding schools, such as the Ecole Spéciale Militaire, which was first housed in a wing of the magnificent palace of Fontainebleau. At this palace, built for the Renaissance King François I as a grand hunting lodge, representations of horses decorated the rooms and the grounds. The most valuable work of art dedicated to horses was the renowned fresco by Francesco Primaticcio, painted in 1541–44, of *Alexander Taming the Horse Bucephalus*. After the thirteen-year-old Alexander tamed Bucephalus, they conquered much of the known world together, from

Greece to Egypt and India. Although Bucephalus is believed to have been a black horse, in this fresco, like Pegasus, he is depicted as white.

The Crown of Charlemagne

During the preparations for the invasion of Britain, Napoleon paused to show again his love of pomp and theatrical splendour, this time with a lavish ceremony at which he instituted the Légion d'honneur – paving the way for the subsequent restoration of the nobility.

Early in 1804 the discovery of a Royalist plot led to what has been described as one of the blackest deeds in Napoleon's career – the murder of the Duke of Enghien, the Prince of Condé's son. Napoleon, infuriated, decided to take a dramatic stand against the continual Royalist plots by executing one of the leading émigrés. Although his involvement with the conspirators was not proven, the Duke of Enghien was seized at his home in Baden and taken to the chateau at Vincennes, where he was shot in a moat. This act dishonoured Napoleon both at home and abroad.

In 1804 yet another plebiscite was held and an overwhelming majority of more than three million elected Napoleon Emperor. It is said that there were only 3,000 or 4,000 votes against, but as the ballot was not secret these figures have always been disputed. After Napoleon assumed the title of Emperor of the French on 18 May, he renamed the Consular Guard, the Imperial Guard. Its mounted Grenadiers comprised 1,018 troopers – all over five foot nine inches tall. Apart from the trumpeters, who were mounted on grey horses, all the men rode heavy black horses, mostly of the Norman or Anglo-Norman breeds.

The ceremony of the coronation on 2 December gave Napoleon a chance to extend his much-acclaimed military reviews and stage a royal pageant of startling proportions, with a parade of what was said to be some 5,000 horses. To stop them slipping, over thirty-seven cartloads of river sand were scattered along the muddy parts of the route. Despite the fact that the numbers in the procession had been limited so it would not take longer than an hour to pass through the freezing winter streets, there were still twenty-five carriages drawn by 152 horses, which were followed by six regiments of cavalry in full dress. The imperial carriage, drawn by eight horses, and attended by twenty squadrons of cavalry, drove through over a mile of streets lined with infantry soldiers, standing two deep. The horses pulling the imperial carriages were the same colour and size – eight for the Emperor's carriage and eight dappled greys for the carriage of the Empress. The aristocratic General Caulaincourt, already part of Napoleon's entourage, became the Master of the Horse. He insisted on buying 140 new horses at the high price for the time of 1,300 francs apiece. Bedecked with white plumes, plaited ribbons, cockades of red and gold and harnesses of red Morocco with the bronze fittings matt-gilded, the Emperor's horses were driven by a coachman appropriately called Caesar.

One of Napoleon's own grey horses was so well trained that he kept his place in the parade without being ridden or led. Covered in a lavish red-velvet jewelled saddle and blanket, the riderless horse projected an imperial presence. There were further reminders of *Egypte française* throughout the proceedings. Even the ancient cathedral doors were covered by a triumphal arch bearing the arms of the Emperor and ornamented with pyramids. The Mamelukes, too, were represented. When he arrived at the ancient cathedral of Notre Dame, Napoleon's heavy red coronation robes slowed his pace as he walked solemnly to the new crimson throne of France. Two gigantic orchestras, drowned by the roar of cannon, struck up martial music and the ceremony began.

Pope Pius VII did not perform the actual crowning, his brief was only to anoint and bless the imperial couple. Napoleon proudly crowned himself with the newly made wreath of golden oak and laurel leaves. After pronouncing the oaths of office on a Bible on the throne, the choir of 300 sang, and the crowds in the audience shouted '*Vive l'Empereur!*' Napoleon murmured to his brother Joseph, 'If only our father could see us now!'

Until then there had only been two emperors in Europe, a Habsburg in the West and a Romanov in the East. They did not like being joined by a third. The British government, refusing to recognise any post-revolutionary French titles, went on referring to the Emperor as 'General Bonaparte'. George III was more than mildly surprised to receive a letter claiming a brotherly relationship and to be called '*mon frère*' by the man who was known throughout his kingdom as 'Boney the ogre' or 'Little Boney'.

While some called Napoleon an upstart, others felt the coronation went against the spirit of the Revolution, which forbade 'all outward signs which imply distinctions of birth'. In Germany, when he heard of the Emperor's coronation, Beethoven tore the dedication page from his Sinfonia Grande Napoleon Bonaparte and renamed it the Eroica – to celebrate the memory, not the glory, of a man he had once so admired.

A successful French officer on the battlefield now had to acquire the grace of a courtier and, like his horse, he had to be trained. Napoleon had the *Etiquette du palais* printed as a guide to the daunting grandeur of the newly created Court. Generals were obliged to wear dress swords and silk stockings (instead of boots and sabres), perfect the art of proffering a bow and learn to dance in skin-tight breeches and brocade coats glittering with gold thread, embroidery and orders. A large number of the new courtiers were never at ease in their freshly purchased finery.

Among the wives who were part of the new court but who would not have been welcomed at the Versailles of old was a former washerwoman, the wife of Marshal François Lefebvre, an ex-sergeant and the son of a miller from Alsace. She never lost her common and direct manners. Nicknamed 'Madame Sans-Gêne', her character was fictionalised in a successful play.

One marshal with lowly origins, who particularly excelled both at Court and in battle, was Jean Lannes, who was cordially detested by Napoleon's friend and brother-in-law Murat. Indeed, while the generals and marshals seemed to work well as a military team, peace often reduced them to bickering. The son of a Gascon farmer and livery-stable keeper with little education, Lannes, whom Madame Junot said 'stormed a fortress more easily than a woman', became one of Napoleon's most intimate friends.

Red-headed Michel Ney, who rose from being a cooper's son, was known as the 'bravest of the brave'. With his powerful body, weather-beaten face and crumpled clothes, this passionate, quick-tempered man could be brash. In Spain he fell out with André Masséna, the son of a wine merchant from Nice who also rose through the ranks to become a general of immense talent. Wellington later said that 'the ablest after Napoleon was, I think, Masséna.' But Napoleon gave Ney rare approbation: 'I have known men more loyal, but none more brave.' Ney and Masséna, too, had to put on buckled dancing shoes.

Re-creating a ruling dynasty in the very land where a reigning monarch had been executed, and where the people had sworn their hatred of kings, was paradoxical. Napoleon granted an amnesty to thousands of exiles and more and more people started to move away from the Revolution and return to observing protocol. Royal customs resurfaced as the Empress Josephine started to be attended by ladies-in-waiting.

Imperial etiquette was not restricted to palaces, but spread to the imperial stables. Horse adornment was dictated by position. Gradually the old custom of domestics grading themselves according to the ranks of their masters crept back throughout Napoleon's palaces from the kitchen to the stables. While imperial bees were embroidered on to everything from the coronation cushion to the royal robes and curtains, the leather-makers were hard at work embossing bees on to harnesses, straps and saddles, ready to be gilded. Just as the majestic fleur-de-lis was the symbol of the Bourbons, the humble bee became the emblem of the Emperor. The bee, the badge of industry and power and the token of some of the pharaohs of Lower Egypt, was adopted by Napoleon at the time of the coronation, under the impression that bees had been the badge of Childéric, father of Clovis. Like Charlemagne and other ruling houses of Europe, he took the spread eagle as the heraldic insignia of France. An unusual choice was green for the imperial liveries, a colour then thought to be unlucky. The crown was stamped on Napoleon's personal property – from attaché cases to carriages and horses, who had the imperial crowned-laureated letter 'N' branded on the left near side of their hindquarters.

As well as an emblem Napoleon had to have a saint who bore the same name. The only saint called Napoleon was associated with a riding accident. In 1218 St Napoleon, then a young man, died after falling from a horse, but was miraculously revived by St Dominique and went on to live a holy life. Napoleon did not like anyone remarking on his riding mishaps. As Madame Rémusat wrote: 'He had several falls which were never mentioned, because it would have displeased him,' – so the coincidence of Saint Napoleon and the Emperor Napoleon falling from horses was unfortunate.

The dashing Murat and the dignified and aristocratic Caulaincourt were the two men Napoleon relied most on to keep up the massive new stables of France. Caulaincourt's wide duties included taking charge of the imperial horses, equipages, despatch riders and orderly officers. His concern for the animals in his care sometimes made him lean out of his carriage – which usually followed Napoleon's – to order the coachmen to slow down in order to spare the horses. As well as taking the orders of the day, he organised the transportation services and planned journeys for the household and, in time of war, the administrative headquarters.

The amount of travelling Napoleon did was unusual for the time.

To ensure that his rule coincided with the rebirth and reorganisation of national industries, he often made visits to factories, encouraging them with patronage and subsidies. After his coronation as emperor, he did not neglect to visit Boulogne, where his army remained camped along the coast in day-to-day readiness to embark on a flotilla of gunboats, sailing packets, scallops, bomb-ships and other transports to cross the Channel to England.

The French coronation was to be followed four months later by one in Italy. So hectic was the time between the two coronations that Napoleon gave himself just two days' holiday. During one of these days he gave his entourage the slip and made a nostalgic return to his old school at Brienne, where he wandered with his Arabian horse through the gardens and explored the buildings. At ten a.m. he started galloping furiously through fields, woods and villages, retracing the footsteps of *l'arrière-cadet de Buonaparte*. After searching for three hours, Caulaincourt found him. The animal was frothing at the mouth, covered in sweat, blood coming from his nostrils. Caulaincourt estimated that in that brief time Napoleon had ridden for at least fifteen leagues.

Although the Treaty of Lunéville had stipulated the independent status of the north Italian Cisalpine Republic, Napoleon held a grand coronation in St Ambrose cathedral in Milan on 26 May, at which he crowned himself with the ancient iron crown of the Lombards and made his stepson Eugene Viceroy. This ancient crown, made in 625, was alleged to include one of the nails which had pierced the hand of Jesus Christ when on the Cross. It had not been worn since the coronation of Charles V in the sixteenth century.

Immediately the Austrians ordered armies to Italy and the Tyrol. Then Britain, in an effort to divert Napoleon's troops from invading the English coast, made yet another more powerful coalition. Austria joined the Anglo-Russian alliance, along with Sweden and Naples. Prussia, however, still remained aloof.

8

Austerlitz and Jena

I've seen the Emperor – soul of the world – leave
the town on a reconnaissance expedition; it is
indeed a marvellous sensation to see such a man,
sitting on his horse at this concentrated point,
and spreading his dominion over the whole world.

HEINRICH HEGEL,
Letters

From his spies and diplomats Napoleon knew that the Habsburgs, Romanovs and Hohenzollerns who occupied the thrones of Europe were a mediocre lot. None of them was very bright. Napoleon referred to the occupant of the Austrian throne as 'this skeleton Francis II, whom the merit of his ancestors put on the throne'. However, he was more cautious about the Tsar of Russia, the unpredictable twenty-eight-year-old Alexander. He was known to have an almost childlike desire to please, was easily influenced and quick to change sides, alliances and attitudes – as well as having a leaning to unusual religious practices. The pride and autocratic attitudes of his Romanov ancestors had been tempered by a liberal education. Brought up by his grandmother, Catherine II, who had steeped him in Rousseau and other philosophers of the Enlightenment, he had intended to bring in reforms but seldom had the tenacity to carry them through. Since he had ascended the throne in 1801, after the murder of his father Tsar Paul, Alexander had sided with Austria and England.

The only way that France could beat Austria and Russia was to strike immediately. If Napoleon wasted time, the two forces would unite and overpower him. Napoleon needed to destroy the Austrians before the huge Russian army joined them. He postponed the invasion of England until the winter, placed himself at the head of his army, which he renamed the Grande Armée, and marched away from England, east towards the Danube. Already the advance Russian army under Mikhail Kutuzov, the gnarled old bulldog of a Field-Marshal whose reputation had been made in the war against Turkey, was steadily marching south.

With manic excitement Napoleon fired off remarks such as: 'I plan to have 200,000 men in Germany', 'I will march on Vienna', 'I have nothing more to fear from Austria.' His tactic, which he was to utilise again and again, was rapidity of movement and a surprise invasion before an enemy could mobilise and regroup its forces. Unless he acted with speed against the new coalition of Austria, Britain and Russia, he predicted that he would find 'One hundred thousand Russians in Poland, paid for – horses, guns, and all – by England'. A letter was sent to Austria stating, 'there is no choice left but to repel force by force'.

Unhampered by heavy baggage or supply trains, Napoleon's efficient, mobile army marched at unprecedented speed – some reports put it as high as twenty-five miles a day. The frantic pace told on some of the horses and the losses were alarming. Well trained they might be, but they were not used to such long, fast marches. Too many were kept saddled all night in readiness for a sudden attack. Some developed open sores, others dropped out, a few died. While a deep bond between horse and man often developed, this, alas, was not always the case. The men who felt affection for their horses were seen carefully grooming their animals and sharing their bread rations with them – even sleeping with them. Finding straw for horses to lie down on at night was a rare bonus. Seasoned soldiers had the routine of bivouacking down to a fine art, sleeping in their clothes and improvising shelter by making instant tents out of their coats propped up on muskets. Napoleon's insistence on his soldiers travelling light so they could move rapidly across vast distances meant that they carried few comforts.

At its zenith the imperial cavalry was made up of more than sixty regiments. Each regiment was a basic cavalry unit, comprising 500 men, organised into squadrons and troops. The regimental command of most units was nearly identical to that of an infantry unit. Cavaliers were armed with a sabre and a pistol or carbine, and, with the exception of the Cuirassiers, were trained to fight on foot, on horseback and as mounted infantry. Napoleon always stressed that cavalry units were not interchangeable, that the Cuirassiers, Dragoons and Hussars formed three different arms. Officers of these units, he said, should never shift from one to another.

The Chasseurs were light cavalry, trained for long-range reconnaissance and pursuit over any sort of terrain from mountains to plains. Their function was to enlighten and to protect the army. The men of the Dragoons rode heavy, cob-type horses and were used in various roles including flank guards and charges; the Lancers were mounted on lighter horses and specialised in quick assault charges and fast flanking manoeuvres; the Hussars also rode light, fast horses and specialised in sudden attacks in battle as well as long-range reconnaissance and pursuit. In battle the Cuirassiers, armoured in helmets and breastplates, were used in powerful charges.

Both man and animal were taught gymnastic exercises. Each learnt methods of quick recovery, changes of pace, alteration of stride and the charge. While a horse had to learn to adapt to carrying the weight of the rider and his weapons, each rider had to adjust to different horses and learn to keep his balance in battle. The Chasseurs and Hussars were taught to ford rivers by swimming with their horses, grasping their manes with one hand and holding their carbine well above the water with the other. Neither horse nor man was burdened with heavy baggage or weapons. The weight of each man's carbine and bayonet was no more than six pounds, while their two pistols weighed scarcely one pound each and the sabre no more than three pounds. The only other military hardware they carried were a lance, scaled epaulettes and an iron cross on their shakos. They slept in their uniforms.

Smaller pieces of armour continued to be used. So dangerous was it for the men in the cavalry regiment, the Cuirassiers, that Napoleon ordered them to wear metal breastplates and helmets, though the horses were completely without protection, their legs at the mercy of foot soldiers. The quickest means of throwing an opponent was to hamstring his horse, cutting through the tendons in the legs so the animal collapsed. Other hazards included tripping on potholes dug by the enemy and camouflaged with sods of earth, stumbling over dead and dying horses, slipping on the entrails of animal corpses, getting bogged down in mud, being lamed by hidden nails and spikes. Slashing the head of the animal and slicing through its halter and reins could also unseat an opponent. The list goes on.

Moving thousands of horses to distant battlefields required enormous amounts of food and water. Sufficient provisions could not be carried, so food was gathered wherever possible, making armies unpopular with local people; even when produce was not plundered but requisitioned and paid for, this resulted in shortage for the locals and money was little compensation. Some cavalrymen travelled with reaping hooks, scythes and whetstones and collected grass from hedge bottoms. Animals on active service demanded more than straw, bad hay, oats and corn – they needed green food. (Wellington delayed his 1813 campaign in Spain and Portugal because, after their sea voyage, the horses were not fit for battle until nourished on green food for about a month.)

The Grande Armée made its way across Germany in the direction of the Rhine to the sound of the heavy plod of weary horses, the jingle of harness and the smell of sweat and wet leather. It was the largest army that Napoleon had ever moved. During his first Italian campaign he had mustered between 25,000 and 40,000 men, at the Battle of Marengo he had 60,000. Now his army was more than three times that number. Ahead of the foot soldiers, like a moving screen, rode the newly formed Cavalry Reserve led by Murat. Despite deficiencies in numbers, this reserve now comprised 21,000 men – about 10 per cent of Napoleon's army – and was amazingly versatile. Apart from two divisions of Cuirassiers and five of Dragoons, it included brigades of light cavalry all trained to be skilful both on the battlefield and in pursuit of the enemy.

Napoleon planned in advance every move his troops made; he knew accurately the level of the terrain, the depth and width of every river, the places where his huge army and those of his enemies might go. He reminded his generals to ensure their men were trained to cross rivers. Wherever he marched huge maps were unrolled and laid out flat in a tent. His valet Constant described his reliance on them: 'During the three or four days preceding a fight the Emperor passed most of his time stretched out on large maps, into which he thrust pins with heads of wax of various colours.' Napoleon's vigilance kept everyone alert. Instructions had been sent off for 'two portable boxes, divided into compartments . . . so one can find out at a glance, with the help of cards, the movements of all the Austrian troops, regiment by regiment, and battalion by battalion.'

When inspecting his troops he referred often to a pocketbook in which he had recorded the numbers of men, horses and equipment in each regiment. One morning, while looking at possible army positions,

Napoleon saw the light cavalry of his Guard and realised immediately that men and horses were missing. Nothing escaped him. Calling over the general in charge he reprimanded him: 'Your regiment is down in my notes as having 1,200 men, and although you have not yet had an engagement with the enemy, you have not more than 800 horsemen there. What has become of the others?' Although a satisfactory answer was given, he was not pleased.

On 20 October 1805 the Grande Armée won an outstanding victory over the Austrians, whose army surrendered at Ulm. Napoleon gave priority to the infantry and the cavalry – using heavy cavalry rather like tanks in the Second World War, while the light cavalry was designed to engage in light reconnaissance and pursuit of a fleeing army. Winter had set in earlier than usual and the horses suffered terribly from the cold. Napoleon wrote to Josephine about 'being wet through every day for a week, and my feet frozen with cold'. He went on to say that he had 'destroyed the Austrian army, and captured 60,000 prisoners, 120 guns, over 90 flags, and more than 30 generals'. The edge was quickly taken off the victory with news of the French defeat in the Battle of Trafalgar, near Cadiz. Eighteen French ships of the line had been lost and the French admiral taken prisoner. Britain's supremacy of the seas had been confirmed. Napoleon, though would show that he was master of the continent – even though an invasion of England was now out of the question. His victory at Ulm had been so great that he could regard a catastrophe at sea as of secondary importance.

On 13 November Murat and Lannes seized the main bridge over the Danube at Vienna and French troops entered the Austrian capital. Napoleon's forces were everywhere, both overtly and under cover. Hooded men on black horses with muffled hooves penetrated enemy camps at night, while bilingual officers interrogated peasants. The Russians converged around Olmutz, while Napoleon concentrated his troops around Brün in an enormous rectangle about fifty by

An unflattering portrait of Napoleon mounted which appeared in England.

seventy miles. The Russians started to advance on Napoleon's right flank in an attempt to encircle him and cut off his lines of communication. On 2 December the two armies came face to face at Austerlitz on the first anniversary of Napoleon's coronation at Notre Dame. Again temperatures were so low that soldiers had to break the ice on ponds with cannon shot.

This was the battle at which Marengo – according to the inscription on his hoof at St James's Palace, as well as the notices when he was exhibited in the Waterloo Rooms in 1823 and later at the RUSI Museum – was ridden by Napoleon. The *Animals' Who's Who* says that Marengo was credited with saving Napoleon 'from capture by sprinting away from a surprise encounter with enemy cavalry the night before the battle of Austerlitz', a story which is repeated in other books. But in *Le Registre d'Ordre du Grand Ecuyer* and *Le Registre du Contrôle de l'Equipage de Selle* no horse by the name of Marengo is listed as being in Napoleon's stables at that time. The horse which Napoleon rode at Austerlitz, according to French records, was the sprightly Ali. But as he and Marengo were both grey Arabs the confusion may not be surprising – in *War and Peace* Tolstoy described Napoleon at Austerlitz: 'Napoleon was standing a little in front of his marshals, on a little grey Arab horse, wearing the same blue overcoat he had worn through the Italian campaign.' The problem of distinguishing which horse Napoleon rode in which battle is not made any easier by looking at the official paintings. So many horses, so many different stories, so many different images on canvas. The light grey horse depicted in the commemorative painting by the studio of Carle Vernet could, indeed, be Marengo or Ali or any one of Napoleon's many little Arabs. Napoleon awarded Vernet the Légion d'Honneur for his huge canvas of the Battle of Austerlitz as well as his vast painting of the Battle of Marengo. Both now hang at Versailles.

On the eve of the battle precise instructions were delivered by an aide to each corps, setting out the position and time at which they were to gather. At seven o'clock on the morning of the battle Napoleon met his marshals at headquarters to issue fresh orders. The fog was so thick that the men could see only ten paces in front of them. Then the legendary 'sun of Austerlitz' rose with uncommon brilliancy – considered such an omen of victory that it was immortalised by Victor Hugo in *Les Misérables*. Caulaincourt was near Napoleon, ready to ride into battle with him and ready to surrender his horse to his master should the need arise. Before the battle Napoleon, riding along the lines, excited the enthusiasm of his soldiers and was received with prolonged cheers of '*Vive l'Empereur!*' Then the French line stood silent, immobile, with ordered arms, ignoring what was about to break when the first shot was fired. Waiting for the sun to thaw the slushy layer of snow, Napoleon continued to pull his troops on the right flank of the battlefield a little into the rear.

The Tsar, a poor horseman, mounted on a chestnut stallion with a docked tail, waited nervously. Neither he nor his horse had ever been on a battlefield before – only on military parades in St Petersburg. His handsome brother, the Grand Duke Constantine, headed eighteen squadrons of cavalry of the elite Russian Imperial Guard, composed of the most brilliant young men of the Russian nobility, all on black horses in dazzling white uniforms. The Emperor of Austria, like the Tsar, stood in the background.

Who would make the first move? Another hour passed. And another. The Tsar, keyed up and impatient, told General Kutuzov, whose motto was 'Time and Patience', to get on with the attack. When the Tsar asked Kutuzov, 'Why haven't you begun your advance?' the old General, who was against precipitate action, replied: 'Your Highness, I am waiting for all the columns of the army to get into position.' The angry young Tsar replied: 'But we are not on the Empress's Meadow, where we do not begin a parade until all the regiments are formed up!' 'Your Highness! If I have not begun, it is because we are not on parade, and not on the Empress's

Meadow. However, if such be Your Highness's order.'

The Russian troops moved forward and rushed down the hill. As the sun broke through the fog the French saw immense numbers of enemy troops across the plain – some of the Russian forces were going down the valley to the ponds and lake.

As the battle started, the noise of cannon balls, the champing of horses' bits, the gunfire, the rattling of swords and the bullets hitting the breastplates of the French Cuirassiers made such an infernal uproar that officers could barely hear the reports and up-to-the-minute information brought to them at a gallop or make their commands understood over the deafening sounds. Many of the Russian regiments lacked horsemen or scouts to carry messages between their leaders during the battle. Slow communication between the different Russian columns was a handicap, whereas Napoleon had trained the Chasseurs à Cheval in all aspects of communication during battle. The ice and cold ensured there was not the usual dust, but the smoke was dense and even though the noise was immense the musicians were playing loudly in the centre of each battalion. On the hill the Tsar's horse reared at the unexpected sounds of gunfire. This horse, which had carried his master at many reviews in Russia, had not undergone the same harsh training for warfare as Napoleon's horses. Napoleon and his horse kept back from the centre so that he could see and control the fighting, give instructions and receive messages from his aides who galloped to and fro. As always, he had a spyglass in one hand.

Although it is not possible to give an account of the progress of the battle, regarded as one of Napoleon's greatest victories, in a few pages, it is relevant here to describe one of the most horrific but magnificent cavalry changes in history. Ten regiments of French horsemen drew up in parallel lines, shoulder to shoulder, stirrup to stirrup, each man with his hands on the bridle, ready to go. The smell of unwashed men mingling with the strong odour of horses and exploding muskets. Restrained and rigid they formed an impenetrable wall. This was Napoleon's cavalry at its peak. The curb chains of the bridles jingled as the horses held back and waited nervously, like their masters, for death or glory. Nerves were steadied, horses snorted, then, at last, the order rang out, '*Charge!*'

Each man put in his spurs. The horses took off to the massive sound of trumpets, which blocked out the roar of the battle, the rallying cries and the loud groans of the dying. The very ground seemed to move as the mass of hooves rumbled forward. Cannons were fired. Soon everything was lost in smoke. Thousands of Russians and Austrians were mown down. It was impossible to step even a few feet without treading on a wounded or dead body. The methods of the Mamelukes were murderously effective.

As horses reared and plunged, some tripped and collapsed on the bodies of fallen comrades. Even if not yet badly hurt, they soon become trapped by the next wave of horses and riders crashing on top of them. Soldiers, crushed under the weight of their fallen horses, tried to slither through the mud on their stomachs, only to have their hands and feet trampled to pieces by thundering hooves. Fanatical soldiers refused to surrender even when unhorsed and fought to the death with sword and pistol. Few of the thousands in that impressive cavalry charge would survive.

Even men lying on the ground scrambled to fire their muskets. The circular leaden balls which they fired flattened during flight so they sliced through their victims and inflicted appalling wounds; the muskets were so difficult to aim that in battle conditions there were usually three misses in every four shots. But while bullets fired from muskets were inaccurate at a hundred paces, they could still kill at over five hundred yards.

From a hill Napoleon's artillery fired incessantly on the Russians and the Austrians, forcing them into a hollow. A few frozen lakes were the only means of escape until French guns thundered cannon balls

General Rapp, Governor of Dantzig, presenting the defeated Prince
Repnin to Napoleon at the Battle of Austerlitz, 1805, by Baron
François Pascal Simon Gérard

down on them, plunging thousands of men and horses into the icy
water. Some froze to death, others sank and quickly drowned. Those
on the edges were gutted by sabres and bayonets. Later, Napoleon
compared the mass drowning to the time, six years earlier, at the
Battle of Aboukir, when 'the sea was covered with turbans'.

Firing ceased at four thirty in the afternoon. In half a day Napoleon
had gained victory and squashed England's Third Coalition. The sun
sank behind the dense clouds and rain began to fall. The phrase *soleil
d'Austerlitz* had brought Napoleon such good fortune that for him it
became a symbol of good luck. Later, he often referred to the battle:

114

'Success in war depends so much on quick-sightedness, and on seizing the right moment. The battle of Austerlitz, which was so completely won, would have been lost if I had attacked six hours sooner.' He gave François Gérard instructions to depict him with 'the calm appropriate to the habit of victory'. The result was the well-known canvas, *The Battle of Austerlitz*.

Confusion and disorder impeded the retreat. The Russians suffered the worst casualties of the day – just under 20,000 killed, missing or badly wounded. Kutuzov silently blamed the Tsar for the catastrophe. In the retreat, the Tsar was found sitting under a tree, where he had burst into tears. Consoled, he then rode with his generals for seven miles to a peasant's hut, where he was soothed with a mixture of camomile, opium and wine.

That night, accompanied by two of his marshals, Napoleon walked through the corpses on the battlefield. One observer wrote:

> Napoleon ordered his entire suite to remain silent, so that we could hear the cries of the wounded. Whenever he heard one of these unfortunates he went to his side, dismounted, and made him drink a glass of brandy from the store which followed him everywhere . . . the squadron of his escort spent the whole night stripping the Russian corpses of their greatcoats, with which to cover the wounded.

To prevent a counter-attack, the cavalry, hounding and harassing, persisted in a ruthless pursuit of the defeated army. Among those in the retreat was the Tsar, who was forced to keep moving for three days until his army reached the safety of Russian territory.

The Tsar was not included in the peace negotiations between the Emperors of France and Austria when they met after the battle in front of a fire in Napoleon's bivouac, 'the sole palace I have lived in for the past two months'. Antoine Gros's canvas of the scene shows

Napoleon's horse as a big chestnut – Roitelet, who was from an English sire and French dam. Napoleon must have changed horses. Ali the swift Arab was ridden during the battle and replaced by the more imposing Roitelet for the meeting. Napoleon had at first taken a dislike to this chestnut horse because at Schönbrunn in 1809, during a review, he had rushed Napoleon into the ranks of the Guard causing injuries to some of the men.

For weeks after on the battlefield the bodies of tens of thousands of men and horses lay in heaps, unburied, as the frosted ground was too hard to dig. Near-freezing temperatures slowed down the usual stench of death from the decomposing bodies, each of which was rolled over by the looters. Only torn clothing was spurned by the peasants, who, as usual, stripped the field of anything that they could cart off – from horseshoes and harnesses to breeches and false teeth. Other scavengers, the crows and ravens, gorged on the flesh of both beasts and men. Eventually the rain came.

Napoleon, quick to take advantage of his spectacular victory, gained control of vast territories. In the Treaty of Pressburg he rearranged frontiers to enfeeble Austria and strengthen his own influence through his south German allies. After seven centuries the Holy Roman Empire was no more. Austria was forced to renounce all influence in Italy and relinquish its historic possessions in south-west Germany. Hanover, an hereditary possession of George III, was handed to Prussia, while other extensive territories in Germany were given to Napoleon's protégés in Bavaria, Baden and Würtemberg – the Duke of Würtemberg was George III's son-in-law. The Confederation of the Rhine – a collection of large states and little principalities – was brought into being with Napoleon as its Protector and soon embraced western Germany.

In 1806 a series of weddings and promotions strengthened Napoleon's position in Europe. The King of Bavaria's daughter, Princess Augusta, was married to his stepson Eugene; the Crown

Prince Charles Frederick of Baden was married to Josephine's niece by marriage, Stephanie de Beauharnais; his brother Louis, who had earlier married Josephine's daughter Hortense, was made King of Holland; his brother Joseph entered Naples at the head of French troops and took the throne from the Bourbons; his sister Elisa (Marianne) was given the principality of Piombino and took control of Lucca as well; his brother Jerome was married to the plain Princess Catherine of Würtemberg and made King of the newly created German state of Westphalia; Joachim Murat was given the Grand Duchy of Berg. Napoleon insisted that even the most remote of his puppet heads of state should set up French-style institutions and adopt the Code Civil.

Over 200,000 soldiers of the Grande Armée remained in southern Germany, along the Rhine. Special funds were issued to each regiment to purchase German remounts, not young ponies or colts, but fully grown horses, at least five years old, strong enough to sustain the gruelling life of a warhorse. The German states, all rich agricultural countries, boasted many magnificent studs specialising in a variety of breeds. Good stallions and mares went south to France to fulfil the continual need for new blood and animals with good pedigrees. But, despite victory opening up this large new horse market, the old problem of a shortage of good mounts remained. Napoleon's anxiety about the actual number of horses in his army can be seen in a defensive letter to his Chief of Staff, written at Saint Cloud in September 1806. He insisted that the numbers were more than had been reported to him. Many animals, he said, had been overlooked:

You estimate that there are 28,000 horses in the Grand Army. But you include in them neither the 4th Dragoons, nor the 20th Chasseurs. You do not count, either, a thousand men who have left Paris and are about to join the army, which will then consist of 30,000 men. But you are wrong if you think that all those are

117

troopers' horses. The officers' horses are included therein; and you know that a lieutenant has two horses, a captain three, a major and a colonel more, which very much increases the number of non-combatants. This, therefore, must be distinguished with greater clearness by setting down the officers' horses in one column and those of the soldiery in another.

In September 1806, ten months after France's momentous victory at Austerlitz, Prussia, uneasy at Napoleon's alliances and high-handed behaviour in Germany, threatened war against France unless its troops were withdrawn beyond the Rhine. Napoleon allowed Josephine to travel with him as far as Mainz and then he headed north to face the advancing army of the newly formed coalition of Russia and Prussia. On 14 October 1806 Napoleon shattered his enemies in the massive twin battles of Jena and Auerstädt. Again at Jena, both at the battle and afterwards, the heroism of the men and horses was outstanding. Napoleon later remarked: 'After Jena, the light cavalry capitalized the victory all on its own.'

Jena was another battle in which, according to the RUSI Museum catalogue and many books, including Dorling Kindersley's *Encyclopaedia of the Horse*, Napoleon rode Marengo. But again there is no record in the French archives of a horse with that name at that time. There is a possibility, as noted earlier, that Marengo – who later became such a vivid part of the London scene with his dished face and appealing eyes – may have been a nickname for another horse, possibly Ali, who was listed as a favourite. For at Jena, as at Austerlitz, Napoleon was said to have ridden – among others – Ali and Bacha.

As had happened after Austerlitz, Murat's cavalry covered about twenty-two miles daily, hotly pursuing the retreating Prussian army until it disintegrated. One of the Prussian generals, a former cavalry officer, the rough and uncultivated Lieutenant-General Gebhard von Blücher, was later to avenge himself on Napoleon for the humiliating defeat of Prussia, once the leading military power in Europe. Born in 1842, he had risen through Frederick the Great's army and was the most tenacious and successful Prussian field Commander of the period. Napoleon's armies continued to sweep through Prussia, taking city after city. In October Napoleon slept at Sans Souci, the palace of Frederick the Great. Paying homage to his old hero, he said: 'I would not be here if you were alive.' A few days later he made his entry into Berlin, passing under the monument to Prussia's former glory, the Brandenburg Gate.

When Napoleon was presented with the keys of the city of Berlin, he was mounted on one of the impressive larger horses taken to Germany to be used for ceremonial duties. During the long-drawn-out ceremony, it is said that Napoleon complained of hunger and one of the councillors offered him a slice of moist dark wholemeal bread. He took one mouthful, disliked it and exclaimed that he would give it to the horse whose name was Nickel – saying either '*Bon pour Nickel!*' or '*Pain pour Nickel!*' which became 'Pumpernickel'. Like countless other anecdotes about Napoleon and horses, different versions of the story vie with one another. It is almost impossible to untangle myth from reality. The story is unlikely because no horse called Nickel is listed in the archives in France. Another version is that Napoleon, keenly interested in the diet of his horses, concocted a mixture of molasses and various grains as a treat and dietary supplement. As it had the taste of bread, Napoleon was in the habit of telling his groom to give his horse the same bread mixture that he ate himself: '*Donne le pain pour Nickel*' which ended up sounding like '*Donne le Pain-pournickel*'.

Supplies for the vast and scattered French army were another problem. An order for 85,000 overcoats and 250,000 pairs of shoes was painfully slow in being filled. Another order to equip field hospitals showed an attempt to improvise: 12,000 tents were to be cut up and made into pairs of sheets; another batch of 12,000 tents was to be cut up into 40,000 shirts and pairs of trousers, also for the wounded. Orders from Germany came flooding into Paris: at least 80,000 conscripts were requested, as were 50,000 rations of biscuit a day, bullets and horses and more horses. Although more and more supplies were needed, under Napoleon's direction the army was also becoming more efficient. With foresight he set out to standardize harnesses, saddles and muskets, and the types of artillery wheels were reduced from twenty-two to eight.

Beside a bivouac fire or in a castle, wherever he was, Napoleon received and sent dispatches to sovereigns and officials all over Europe. No subject was too trivial for his attention. He dictated thousands of letters on everything from foreign policy to drains and law reform.

Every victory in Germany was celebrated in champagne, a still relatively unknown drink. French vintners rushed in supplies, seizing the opportunity to set up sales organisations, and Napoleon came to know Jean Rémy Moët. Napoleon's later trips through Epernay on the way to Germany stirred Moët to build a special house for him, complete with gardens and stables modelled on Versailles, near the winery and chalky caves where the bottles were and still are stored. It was only about seventy kilometres from Brienne where Napoleon had been at school.

The closing stages of 1806 were favourable for Napoleon. His forces won a minor victory over the Russians at Pultusk in Poland, but most importantly he had confirmation that he was able to father a child. A courier galloped almost non-stop from Paris with the news. Eleonore Denuelle, who was a 'lectrice' to Caroline Murat, had been a mistress of little importance, organized it appears by the Bonapartes in the hope of proving that Napoleon was not sterile. To show that the lady in question had no feelings for Napoleon, one only has to repeat her jibe that in the middle of the Emperor's caresses she used to push the big hand of the clock beside the bed with her toe, advancing it by half an hour and, by doing so, shortening the session, as Napoleon timed his lovemaking as he did everything else. Nevertheless, on 13 December the Bonapartes had their proof – she gave birth to a boy. The doubts about Napoleon's potency were now laid to rest – until whispers were heard that the baby might have been fathered by the lusty Murat.

A week after hearing of the birth of this child, Napoleon was writing to a Polish beauty, the twenty-year-old Marie Walewska: 'I saw no one but you, I admired no one but you, I want no one but you. Answer me at once.' Married to an ageing regional governor, forty-nine years her senior, Marie Walewska had long hero-worshipped Napoleon; she looked to him to liberate her beloved Poland from Russia and Prussia and to restore Polish independence. Fascinated by her patriotism, which reminded him of his feelings for Corsican independence in his youth, he sometimes started his letters to her, 'Little patriot'. Their affair deepened. Josephine's tearful pleading to her husband to let her join him in Poland was ignored. Although he would not return to Paris until July 1807 – an absence of ten months – another two years would pass until the divorce, which Josephine feared daily, became a reality.

It was not just wife and mistress who were cast aside and replaced. When new imperial horses were acquired, older stallions were put out to pasture or sent to stud farms. Napoleon rode horses not only as machines of war but also for recreation, exploiting them for their power, as well as for showmanship. Wherever he went, there were horses close by ready for him to ride. When long journeys were planned, groups of saddle-horses were tethered at intervals in advance so that Napoleon and his aides had a supply of fresh horses every ten or fifteen kilometres.

9

Brides, Battles and Horses

O, for a horse with wings!

WILLIAM SHAKESPEARE,
Cymbeline

Napoleon's affair with Marie Walewska was disrupted by the advancing Russian army. On 8 February 1807 in the Battle of Eylau, twenty-two miles south of Königsberg, near the east Prussian border, the Russian army nearly beat Napoleon, showing him that he was not invincible. Only the French cavalry saved the army from collapse. During a snowstorm, Napoleon threw in Murat's cavalry against the Russians and over 10,000 cavalrymen made a single thundering charge. The casualties on both sides were horrific; whole battalions and regiments were annihilated. Although Napoleon presented Eylau as another victory for France, it was a massacre without a real result, just a stalemate with over 15,000 French soldiers lying in the snow, dead or wounded.

Napoleon decided to wait until the spring before he attacked the Russians again, so the Grande Armée was forced to endure the shocking north European winter under canvas. As well as the terrible cold there was not enough food for the horses who began tearing straw from roofs in an attempt to assuage their hunger. Many horses also developed sores on their backs; having lost so much weight, their saddles, saddle-cloths and harnesses became loose and caused irritation. Another problem was the dearth of stables in which they could shelter.

During this long wait Napoleon lived with Marie Walewska – a departure from his behaviour with his earlier mistresses who had been slotted into his usual busy schedule. But he did not forget Josephine. On 14 June 1807, on the seventh anniversary of the Battle of Marengo, after he finally routed the Russians at Friedland, Napoleon wrote to Josephine: 'The entire Russian army is in flight. Friedland is a victory worthy of her sister victories Marengo, Austerlitz and Jena, a name to become equally famous and glorious among my people.' Tsar Alexander broke his alliance with the English and signed a treaty with Napoleon, making him the pivotal figure in Europe.

In two weeks Napoleon had a meeting with Tsar Alexander and Prince Frederick William of Prussia in a tented, beflagged raft at Tilsit. With his usual theatrical flair, Napoleon arranged for the raft to be constructed and moored midstream on the River Niemen (now often on maps as the Neman) so they could talk together in a neutral spot midway between their armies. As Napoleon travelled to meet his foes from Austerlitz and Friedland, he demonstrated that he was a fearless rider by galloping at his usual speed. While the Tsar, on a much larger horse, maintained the pace, Frederick of Prussia – whom Napoleon considered a bore and a dullard, too influenced by his wife – could not keep up, lagging pitifully behind. After this humiliation Frederick was left on the banks of the river, while Napoleon and Alexander boarded the fantasy raft for the first day of negotiations.

One side of the raft was little more than a cabin for the staff and relatively plain, while the other side contained a larger pavilion with fine carpets draped on wooden railings, recalling *Egypte française*.

Napoleon in 1809 by Jean-Baptiste Debret.
The painting is now in Versailles.

Over the entrance of the larger pavilion, facing the German side of
the river, was a large gilded 'N' encircled by swags of laurel leaves,
while facing the Russian side was an enormous 'A'. Frederick's
monogram was missing.

Alexander agreed to support Napoleon's hegemony in Europe,
while Napoleon, in turn, agreed to leave the Tsar a free hand east of
the River Niemen. Napoleon's handling of Alexander was so masterly
that the two men became friends and Alexander no longer objected to
the fact that most of Italy, Holland, Belgium and central Germany
was made up of vassal states ruled either by Bonapartes or sovereigns
who carried out Napoleon's orders.

The Treaty of Tilsit allowed Napoleon to put in place his mighty economic blockade against Britain with the words: 'All trade with the islands of Britain is forbidden.' By banning the importation of British goods Napoleon would defeat 'this nation of shopkeepers' economically. He reasoned that if England could not sell its wares, it would be beset by unemployment and the workers would rebel. Many English factories did close and hardships resulted, but British manufacturers also had the advantage that cheaper goods from the continent were not flooding the market. One flamboyant Russian-born financier, established in the city of London, John Julius Angerstein, made a fortune despite the war. His grandson would be the owner of the horse known as Marengo.

When Napoleon returned to Paris at the end of July, after nearly a year's absence, he had added seventy million people to the French Empire. The following month his birthday was celebrated with a mass at Notre Dame and, of course, military parades. Egypt was not forgotten. He mixed an Oriental-potentate-like ceremonial with the old tradition, grandeur and etiquette of France. Just as the jackets of the Mamelukes glittered with gold and silver embroidery and Napoleon's equerries and pages wore silks and velvets, his horses had immaculately brushed coats and finely plaited harnesses. The colours in the fringed and embroidered saddle-cloths often matched the beribboned manes. Many paintings of Napoleon mounted on grey Arabs show this introduction of the Egyptian style into European horsemanship.

A series of receptions, balls, fêtes and entertainments celebrated the return of the conquering hero, attended by returning *émigrés*, the bourgeoisie, the *arrivistes*, the *parvenus*, the soldiers promoted through the ranks, the gifted commoners, the scientists, the artists and the financiers. Amidst the splendour and glamour, visitors were received in order of precedence and with strict – and boring – court etiquette. The French author Jean Tulard says that 79 per cent of the new nobility were generals and other men in Napoleon's vast military machine, while the remainder were bureaucrats and state officials. A little over half of these, 57 per cent, were from the solid, well-educated middle class, while 20 per cent had risen from humble origins. The old nobility made up the remaining 23 per cent. An example of the new post-revolutionary titles was that of 'baron', awarded to the surgeon who gave the present meaning to the word *ambulance*. Dominique-Jean Larrey was ennobled for establishing the world's first army ambulance services with stretchers and light carts to take the wounded from battlefields.

The next year, 1808, was the zenith both of Napoleon's Empire, which now included Portugal and Spain, and of his reign. Nothing reflected this more than the Salon of that year, in which David's impressive *Coronation* canvas, Gros's *Battle of Eylau* and many other paintings showed the leading artists of the French School at their best. Napoleon's patronage had raised the arts to a standard no other nation could then equal. In under ten years, like Napoleon, the arts had risen from the chaos and poverty of the Revolution to undisputed leadership in Europe. But from then on the slide started, running parallel with French losses in Portugal and Spain.

When the Portuguese refused to stop importing British goods they found their country invaded by French troops. The royal family fled to Brazil. Napoleon cunningly enticed the slow-witted Charles IV of Spain to abdicate in favour of his brother Joseph, who was declared King of Spain on 6 June 1808. At the same time Murat moved from Berg to occupy the throne at Naples. Some of Napoleon's sovereigns were shifted around as if they were government officials.

The only time Napoleon presided over all the sovereigns from his vassal states together was in October 1808 at Erfurt, one of Germany's oldest cities. Nearly three weeks of festivities – hunts, balls, dinners and theatrical performances – were staged to mark this congress, which was also his second meeting with the Tsar whom he planned to make his brother-in-law. A subtle proposal was put forward for the hand of Alexander's capricious younger sister the Grand Duchess Catherine, known for her almond-shaped eyes and strong views. Unbeknown to Napoleon, the Tsar's relationship with her was close enough to provoke gossip of incest. Alexander was horrified at the idea of such a union. He procrastinated, arguing his need to consult with his mother the Dowager-Empress and, of course, his sister. Alexander's first enthusiasm for Napoleon was on the wane. On a political level, too, he was angry that Napoleon had created the Grand Duchy of Warsaw. So instead of a Romanov bride, Napoleon was given a Romanov horse. The Tsar presented him with Tauris – a little grey with a white mane and cocked tail – noted in the archives as a Russian horse, but usually said to be of Persian origin.

A month after Erfurt Alexander slighted Napoleon by announcing that his sister was to marry the Prince of Oldenburg. As the Tsar's other sister, Anna, was only fourteen, he had firmly shut the door on Napoleon becoming a member of the Romanov family. Meanwhile Josephine hung on in Paris as Napoleon's wife – until Metternich started plotting to bring about his marriage to Marie Louise, the daughter of the Emperor of Austria.

In 1809 most of the Grande Armée was in Spain, which, according to Wellington, because of difficult battle conditions and lack of forage, was a 'grave for horses'. Some of the French regiments were recalled yet again to face Austria when they attacked Bavaria in an attempt to lure the German states to rise against France. Napoleon's triumphant finale was the Battle of Wagram, north-east of Vienna, fought during a heatwave on 5–6 July 1809. The 23,000 French cavalry in the battle were used powerfully. Later, Napoleon said:

Cavalry is useful before, during and after a battle. An army superior in cavalry will always have the advantage of covering its movement well, of being always well instructed or well aware of

Napoleon having his foot bandaged, by Pierre Gautherot.
The painting is now in Versailles.

the movements and to engage itself only as far as it wishes. Without cavalry the battles are without results. The defeats will be of little consequence and its effects will not be decisive.

On the eve of the fighting Napoleon spent the entire night riding Ali as he reconnoitred, and then he rode him for most of the battle. This is contrary to the information in London and elsewhere. On the silver lid of the hoof in St James's Palace we are told that Napoleon rode Marengo, but his name cannot be found in any French archives or records of the imperial stables for this time. Yet vivid descriptions of Marengo in battle appear in books such as the excellent *Encyclopedia of the Horse* by Elwyn Haitley Edwards (1994): 'Marengo seems to have had an extraordinary constitution. He was swift, handy, absolutely steady under fire, and courageous.'

To celebrate his victory at Wagram, much to the relief of his marshals, Napoleon renamed a dappled grey Arab after the battle. Until then the horse had been known as Mon Cousin, a term he used to address his marshals in letters. There is no indication that Napoleon rode the horse later called Wagram at the battle of the same name, which may indicate that he gave battle names to horses simply to commemorate the battle rather than as a tribute to the role the horse played in it. Jaffa is an even more extreme example; he was named twelve years after Napoleon's victory of that name.

The official paintings by different artists of the Battle of Wagram give clues, but not names, to the horses Napoleon was riding. He is shown on the same grey Arab in three official versions of the campaign, but none records the name of the animal. In Pierre Gautherot's *Napoleon blessé devant Ratisbonne*, the emphasis of the painting is on the Emperor's inflamed right heel because his boots, which he had not removed for three days, pinched a nerve. Impatiently he is trying to remount, his left foot in the stirrup, while his right foot is still in the hands of the surgeon. The horse in the painting is white, but was actually a grey Arab stallion – the same horse as the one in the canvas by Jacques-François Swebach, *Crossing the Danube, before the Battle of Wagram*, and again in the composition by Horace Vernet, *The Battle of Wagram*. It is likely that the artists later visited the imperial stables at the Tuileries to paint the appropriate horse. All evidence points to this horse being Ali. Carle Vernet, the most celebrated animal painter of his day, reflected a little of the current anglomania in his work – he courted fashionable taste with sporting pictures and horse portraits similar to those so popular in England.

In a letter to Josephine, Napoleon summed up the dreadful battle, which left over 30,000 dead and wounded on each side: 'The enemy is flying in disorder, and everything is proceeding according to plan

. . . My losses are high; but the victory is decisive and complete. We have taken more than 100 guns, 12 flags, and a number of prisoners. I am sun-burnt.'

Not only were many horses lost in the battle, a large number were also becoming unfit. Bad shoes meant lame horses. On campaign shoeing had to be done more frequently because rough roads and hard ground caused irregular wear on hooves, damaging them excessively. Hooves grow about half an inch a month and need to be reshod every four to six weeks. If a horse was reshod more often, not enough hoof would have grown for the iron nails to be rehammered into new horn. Corns are formed by ill-fitting shoes and have to be dug out. The horse then has to be rested for a few days. So when a horse lost the same shoe twice in a week he was ready neither for marching nor for battle. Horseshoes were so scarce that soldiers were often seen scavenging in the aftermath of a battle to pull or chisel them off dead horses, although they were unlikely to fit their own horses and needed to be heated and altered for that purpose. Each battalion travelled with a forge cart and an able farrier, but many roads, tracks and paths were so stony and potholed that the bulky carts could not travel on them, thus preventing blacksmiths from getting near the cavalry regiments to make quick repairs to stop lameness during an advance. Napoleon liked to feel that he knew when every horse in a cavalry squadron needed to be reshod and how much it cost.

In 1809 a new system of marking his personal horses was introduced into the stables. As well as the imperial N surrounded by a laurel leaf and crown, each horse was to have its number from the register burnt on to its flank. Order number 561 dated 30 March 1809 states: 'I would also like to ask your excellency to give the order to have some marks made (when I say marks I mean numbers). The N can be useful but numbers are essential for the keeping of the registers and the N is not useful for the description and recognition of

The Battle of Wagram in July 1809 by Horace Vernet.
The painting is now in Versailles.

horses.' This was approved, with the proviso that they must independently be marked on the left rump with an 'N'. It is unlikely that the numbers were allocated arbitrarily as Napoleon had a great sense of order, but whether the numbering relates to the date of arrival into the stables is not clear, although it appears as if it may be, since Ali, who came from Egypt in 1799, is number 71, Tauris, who arrived at the end of December 1809, is 902, and Jaffa, who was purchased in Turkey in August 1808 and arrived in the stables early in 1811, is number 1992. Another example of Napoleon's interest in numbers dates from 1805, when he introduced what was then a unique system of street numbering. He directed that all houses in new streets in Paris be numbered even on the right side and odd on the left, starting from the Seine – before that street numbering had been random. Although Napoleon's system spread all over the world, his horse numbering did not. The British continued to engrave the numbers of their horses on their hooves.

For a while, though, most of Napoleon's personal horses, with their new numbers burnt on their flanks, stayed in Paris. After Wagram, apart from Spain and Portugal, there were no major French battles on the continent. Maria Walewska's pregnancy (her fidelity was never in doubt) confirmed Napoleon's confidence that he could produce a legitimate heir. He divorced Josephine just before Christmas 1809 and began the search for a royal bride.

His second marriage, to Marie Louise of Austria, daughter of the Emperor Francis and niece of Louis XVI and Marie Antoinette, was a further step in changing his image. Marriage by proxy took place in Vienna on 11 March 1810. Napoleon, overawed by his acceptance into the Habsburg family, wanted to make everything perfect for the arrival of his bride and enquired into every smallest detail concerning her, 'as though he had nothing else to think about' wrote his stepdaughter, Hortense. 'Never before had such luxury been seen as that which prepared the Emperor's marriage.'

Paintings of his victories against Austria, including his greatest triumph, Austerlitz, were tactfully taken down from the palace walls; furniture, jewellery, ornaments were chosen. Horses were selected for her use and stabled at the Tuileries. In the hope of minimising the age difference, the forty-year-old Emperor took waltzing lessons so he would be able to dance with his eighteen-year-old wife from Vienna.

On 28 March, unable to wait, Napoleon dashed to the border to meet his bride. The carriages drew up. He opened the door of the berline, climbed in, embraced his bride and unceremoniously bundled out his sister, Caroline Murat, who was acting as chaperone. The couple finally arrived at the chateau of Compiègne, the newly decorated but ancient palace seventy kilometres north-east of Paris where Joan of Arc was captured by the English in 1430. Leaving the carriage first, Napoleon offered his arm to his bride and led her into the salon, where guests, courtiers and members of the household were assembled. Presentations over, he abandoned etiquette and decorum, took Marie Louise by the hand and led her to her apartment. The guests, expecting her to change and then reappear, waited patiently for an hour. They were beginning to think longingly of supper when the Grand Chamberlain came to announce that their majesties had retired. Hunger pangs forgotten the room was soon buzzing with gossip. The couple had gone to bed, even though the civil marriage would not be celebrated for another four days. After the ceremony at Saint Cloud on 1 April there were elaborate and splendid celebrations in the Salon Carré at the Louvre, marking the entry of Napoleon into the cartel of the old royal families of Europe. Marie Louise, who had been brought up to fear and hate the 'Corsican ogre', appeared to respond to his courtship and to become attached to her older husband – despite his continued dalliances.

Perhaps Marie Louise was not such a lucky bride. Until the age of thirty Napoleon had been exceedingly thin with a lean and bony face, but at forty his face had become soft, fleshy and rounded, his body had broadened and his belly was paunchy. His extra weight emphasised his short neck, which had been less noticeable when he was slim. Although his bewitching smile had not disappeared, Napoleon was no longer the dashing *petit corporal* who had captured the heart of the nation. A number of medical authors believe this obesity to be the result of endocrine abnormality caused by the damage to his pituitary gland from his riding accident at Saint Cloud. Otherwise his weight gain is difficult to explain. He was no gourmand; he took a lot of exercise on horseback; he had a passion for being in the fresh air; he ate meals in a hurry; he watered down his wine. Lack of interest in food meant that eating at table was at full gallop – as was lovemaking and most of his pursuits. To relieve the pressure of

Napoleon after the disastrous defeat at the Battle of Leipzig.

such a fast and hectic life, Napoleon rode. Riding was his only true recreation.

Conscious of his status, Napoleon often presented himself in public in reviews, parades, ceremonial occasions and triumphal entries into captured capitals on more impressive and bigger horses. One of these was another grey, Intendant, a big, quiet Normandy horse. Ali appears to have been pushed into the background. Perhaps, like other imperial Arab stallions, he was impregnating mares at the state stud farms. As well as reviving the splendour of the cavalry, Napoleon was expanding France's breeding programme at an unprecedented rate.

No other ruler set a higher example of stamina in the saddle than Napoleon. Although he now relied on well-sprung carriages for long journeys, he always rode closely behind his army. Baron Fain praised his endurance, even though he must have been exaggerating a little:

> He could be untiring, not only on horseback, but also on foot; he sometimes walked five or six hours straight without being aware of it. Returning from Spain in January of 1809, I saw him ride the distance from Valladolid to Burgos (twenty-three leagues) at full gallop in less than a morning. His ride from Vienna to Semmering. . . . The distance was eighteen leagues. He covered it on horseback in the morning, had lunch at Semmering, and returned immediately. He often went on hunts of thirty-six leagues.

10

Campaigning in Russia

Hast thou given the horse strength? Has thou clothed his neck with thunder? . . . He paweth in the valley, and rejoiceth in his strength: he goeth on to meet the armed men. He mocketh at fear, and is not affrighted; neither turneth he back from the sword. The quiver rattleth against him, the glittering spear and the shield. He swalloweth the ground with fierceness and rage . . . He saith among the trumpets, Ha, ha; and he smelleth the battle afar off, the thunder of the captains, and the shouting.

Job 39:19–25

The culmination of Napoleon's hopes for the future occurred on 20 March 1811 when Napoléon-François-Joseph-Charles, King of Rome, was born at the Tuileries. Jubilation in the streets and a 101-gun salute greeted the arrival of the long-awaited heir. Middle-aged but with a young wife and a son, Napoleon's dynasty seemed assured. However, the need for *la gloire* and a creeping degree of megalomania increased his love of grandiose schemes.

The impact of the Continental System, Napoleon's ban on all trade between Britain and the Continent, deepened the growing rift between him and the Tsar during the summer of 1812. Napoleon said that Alexander was 'fickle and feeble'. There were territorial disagreements over the future of Turkey, Poland and Sweden. As well as completing a secret treaty with England and Spain, Alexander, under pressure from Russian merchants, began flouting trade embargoes. As Russia wanted to sell its timbers and hemp to England, Alexander allowed 150 British ships, sailing the American flag, to enter Russian ports with cargoes of British products. Aware that trade embargoes do not work unless they are total and wanting to punish Alexander for his breach of trust, Napoleon declared that he would march his Grande Armée to Moscow – over 1,500 miles from Paris – even though the Peninsular War in Spain and Portugal had become a 'running sore' and had taken the best French troops.

Napoleon assembled around half a million men, many of them conscripts, from each satellite of his vast empire – Poland, Portugal, Bavaria, Croatia, Dalmatia, Denmark, Holland, Naples, north Germany, Saxony, Switzerland, Westphalia, Austria and Prussia. Estimates vary but somewhere between 400,000 and 600,000 men plodded across Prussia to the Russian border accompanied by between 150,000 and 200,000 horses. The 100,000 cavalry horses were boosted by another 30,000 pulling wagons, carts and artillery, as well as horses for the officers and the ambulances. With Napoleon were dozens of horses from his personal stables, but there is no mention of Ali or of Marengo. Documentation shows that Ali remained in France and, accompanied by another horse called Gallipoli, on 17 October 1812 was sent to studs at Le Pin in Normandy and Angers in the Loire.

Determined to improve the quality of horses in France, Napoleon created new studs as well as reviving the old established ones, most of which were located in the rich rural areas of France, such as Orne in

Normandy, Anjou and Navarre. The main centres were Pompadour, Pau and Tarbes. Many of the 1,500-odd stallions in service were either rescued from old stud farms or had been requisitioned or captured from other countries.

Napoleon's aim was to produce a large number of the best cavalry horses, so imported horses were crossed with all breeds. The Arab, he said, was the best horse in the world and he imported as many he could, together with oriental stallions. In so doing he was continuing a well-established royal tradition; the import of Arab stallions into France went back centuries. Charlemagne, a thousand years before, had been given an elephant and some Arab horses.

The two most important studs which were still going strongly at the end of the Louis XVI's reign were Le Pin, founded in 1714, and Pompadour, founded in 1761. Although it is said that eight stallions had arrived from Syria just before the French Revolution to be followed by another twenty-four in 1790, the numbers vary in different reports. Napoleon, with his obsession with order and bureaucracy, established exact record-keeping at the studs.

At dawn on 23 June, Napoleon made a reconnaissance of the banks of the River Niemen with the engineers to decide where to build pontoons and start his invasion. The river was then the border between north-east Prussia and Russia. He returned later on Friedland – named after his earlier victory over the Russians – to make a second reconnaissance by moonlight. As he galloped through the wheat, a hare rushed between the legs of his horse and made him swerve.

The Emperor, whose seat was poor, rolled to the ground but got up so quickly that he was on his feet before I could reach him to give him a hand, [wrote Caulaincourt, his Master of the Horse]. He mounted again without saying a word. The ground was very soft and he was only slightly bruised on the hip. It struck me then that here was a bad omen; nor was I the only one to think so, for the Prince of Neuchâtel instantly seized my hand and said: 'We should do better not to cross the Niemen. That fall is a bad sign.'

It was said that the Romans, who believed in portents, would not have undertaken the crossing of the Niemen. The Emperor began to joke about his fall, but his bad temper and sense of foreboding were obvious. In other circumstances he would have complained about the charger which had caused this foolish accident and would not have spared the Master of the Horse. Although the charger in the well-known story is Friedland, in Dorling Kindersley's *Encylopaedia of the Horse* it is clearly stated under the entry for Marengo that, during the Russian campaign, while Napoleon was riding him, Marengo 'shied at a hare on an icy road, unseating the Emperor. The news of the fall lowered morale.' Other versions of this incident to be found in English publications say the horse involved was Marengo, an example of how stories about Napoleon and horses were distorted in the telling: while the hare still features, as does Napoleon falling off his horse, the wheat field has become an icy road.

Until this moving metropolis of half a million men, horses, wagons, mules, cattle and tents had crossed the three pontoon bridges slung across Niemen, the only sign of life on the other side was the occasional Cossack. It was eight days before every boot and wheel was on hostile soil. Ironically, the second day of the crossing was the fifth anniversary of Napoleon and Alexander's embrace at Tilsit. This time Alexander had made himself Supreme Commander of the Russian army.

Riding in his green, four-wheeled carriage – his travelling office drawn by six regal Limousin horses – Napoleon intended, by rapid manoeuvres, either to force the Russian army into battle or to demoralise it into surrendering without a fight. He did not know that Alexander had said he would never surrender, even though the Russian army was less than half the strength of the French, and was inexperienced and poorly armed despite help from Russia's new ally, Britain. There has always been controversy as to whether or not Alexander's retreat in advance of the invaders was a deliberate policy but by doing so the Russians lured Napoleon further and further into the country's merciless depths, where his troops ran the risk of being encircled and trapped.

Napoleon, lacking his old judgement let alone flair, underestimated Alexander's fanaticism. He believed that Alexander would give in against his mightier army – and if there was not a peaceful settlement then he, Napoleon, would stage one huge and victorious battle. Throughout the Russian campaign, Napoleon sued for peace and was constantly surprised by Russia's reluctance to come to any settlement with him. When he heard that the Russians had evacuated the camp of Drissa, which had taken a year or more to fortify, he thought that he would soon be celebrating victory. But this was not the case.

On Napoleon's army went, towards Moscow. There were dramatic variations in the bright reds, blues and other patches of colour in the long snake of marching men, since the army of each country wore its own uniform, carried its own flags and had its own regimental bands. The men walked, the officers rode. The heat, the bad roads and the lack of food began to tell. Supply wagons were delayed; there was not enough water. The intolerable sweltering summer temperatures and the thirst reminded veterans of that other horrendous campaign in faraway Egypt. One of the first problems was getting the food from the provision wagons at the rear to the men in the front. The wagons and the droves of cattle were at the tail of the march so that their weight would not cut up the roads ahead of the marching men. The men slept out at night, first under the stars and then clouds, as the almost tropical heat was followed by torrential rain. Before the army reached Vilna, many wagons had been abandoned on the roads, stuck in the mud.

Soon the French heard that boats, their alternative means of transporting supplies, had also got into trouble, running aground in the river. Already men had contracted dysentery from ill-made rye bread and 10,000 horses had died from gorging themselves on rank grass. And this was only the beginning.

The Russians were always ahead, laying waste to everything in their wake, drawing the invaders deeper into hostile country. Destroying food and shelter – sometimes even poisoning the water – they left little behind them except smouldering hamlets. Apart from a few Cossacks who continually harassed the French, there was no human presence anywhere. The French trudged on only to find nothing: the inhabitants had fled, taking with them whatever they could and destroying the rest. Hamlets became mirages of deserted streets, hollow smoking houses and empty churches. At the beginning of July the French reached Vilna, where again they found the Russians steadily retreating.

The troops were held up by the dreadful state of Russian roads which slowed down the passage of vital equipment. Even the few roads which were of a reasonable standard were wrecked by the time the vast army of men, horses and vehicles had tramped over them. The low standard of Russian agriculture and the bare-earth strategy made foraging almost futile. Hunger grew. Horses died.

Dispatch riders daily brought copious correspondence from all the capitals of Napoleon's empire. The Emperor was cheered when he read that the United States had declared war on England and that, at last, the French war effort seemed to be improving in Spain.

On 28 July Napoleon was on his horse before daybreak. Later that day the French came face to face with the Russians just before Vitebsk. 'The enemy deployed considerable masses of cavalry, which bore down on the weak regiments of light troops that composed our advance-guard,' wrote Caulaincourt. 'Our cavalry regiments reached them, but could not form up quickly enough to make headway

against the masses of men already engaged with our advance-guard.'
Napoleon spent the day in the saddle, reconnoitring the terrain in
every direction and returning to his tent very late. At dawn the
following day the Russian army had vanished again, as if into thin air.
There were no inhabitants to be found, no prisoners to take, not even
a single straggler to pick up.

Each squadron had a mule carrying an anvil and bellows, followed
by another carrying charcoal and iron. At the close of a day's march
the farriers, 'the sons of Vulcan', attended to the horses but lack of
basic equipment forced this service to deteriorate slowly and horses
became lame because they had no shoes.

By the end of July the cavalry was suffering severely. Caulaincourt
complained of the large number of horses that had died. Many were
lagging behind, wasting away, wandering at the rear and finally
dropping out from weariness and hunger; others painfully followed
their corps, to whom they were a useless burden. Murat agreed with
Caulaincourt and did not hide his concern for the horses. His worries,
though, were ignored. Caulaincourt said that Napoleon did not want
to know about 'reflections that ran counter to his projects, and lent a
deaf ear'. In spite of his uneasiness, Murat used the cavalry with his
usual enthusiasm and Caulaincourt, with some malice, added:

Always at the forefront of the skirmishes, and eager to thrust his
ostrich-plumes and fantastic uniform beneath the very noses of
the Cossacks, he succeeded in ruining the cavalry, ended by
causing the loss of the army, and brought France and the
Emperor to the brink of an abyss.

General Belliard, Murat's Chief of Staff, gathered enough courage to
say to the Emperor: 'Your Majesty must be told the truth. The cavalry
is rapidly disappearing; the marches are too long and exhausting, and
when a charge is ordered you can see willing fellows who are forced to

stay behind because their horses can't be put to the gallop.'

In his memoirs Caulaincourt explained that Napoleon, wanting to reach his prey, paid no attention to caution. He added:

The rapidity of the forced marches, the shortage of harness and spare parts, the dearth of provisions, the want of care, all helped to kill the horses . . . our wagons and all our transport, built for metalled roads and to accomplish ordinary distances, were in no way suitable . . . The first sand we came across overwhelmed the horses; for the loads, instead of being cut down in proportion to the weight of the vehicle and the distance to be covered, had been increased in the notion that the daily consumption would sufficiently lessen them.

The men, lacking everything to supply their own needs, were little inclined to pay any heed to their horses, and watched them perish without regrets, for the death meant the breakdown of the service on which the men were employed, and thus the end to their personal privations.

Much of Napoleon's behaviour was out of character and remained so throughout the campaign. The pituitary dysfunction is one possible reason for this, general illness and urinary problems are others.

Supplies were running dangerously low. The army soon lacked the most basic goods as Cossacks using guerrilla tactics were depleting provisions and equipment further. Horses were not shod, harnesses were in a deplorable state, there were not enough nails or smiths or supplies of suitable iron. Like everything else, most of the forges had been left in the rear, abandoned or lost.

On the eve of his forty-fourth birthday, before even the first light of day, Napoleon was on his horse, hoping to reach a position in advance of the elusive Russian army, which he expected to meet as they approached Smolensk, one of the old Holy Cities. It had taken them fifty-five days to reach it. The next morning he was again galloping at the crack of dawn and at last glimpsed the phantom army. A short and muddled battle at the city gates ended in a swift but bloody victory for Napoleon. Thousands were slain on both sides. Then the city was forsaken and burnt by its own inhabitants, who marched ahead to Moscow. Again Napoleon advanced; again the Russians retreated.

Tolstoy, in *War and Peace*, wrote: 'Napoleon was riding on his cream-coloured English horse, accompanied by his guards ... Napoleon rode on, dreaming of Moscow.'

Meanwhile, in Moscow the Tsar issued a proclamation declaring that no peace would be made with Napoleon. He promised he would not negotiate while a single French soldier remained on Russian soil. The supreme command was handed over to sixty-seven-year-old Mikhail Kutuzov, who wanted revenge on Napoleon for his loss of face and the slaughter of his troops at Austerlitz. No longer in his prime, this depraved but excellent general was too bulky and fat to ride.

The French slowly trod the long road to Moscow, which here was so wide that the infantry and the cavalry could march in files on either side while the artillery and carts occupied the centre. The terrible heat dried up marshes and ponds. Each morning Napoleon changed horses. Sometimes Leonore, sometimes Roitelet, sometimes Embelli, Emir, Tauris or Courtois. If one believes the archives, Ali was not there but at the veterinary school. The RUSI museum in London freely accepted that Marengo was in Russia, but Dr Godefroy de la Roche who wrote a thesis on Napoleon and his horses in 1992 – *Les Chevaux de Napoleon I et les Ecuries Impériales* – and who made extensive searches into all the archives in France, found no reference to a horse called Marengo on the Russian campaign. Nor was Ali on the list of horses which accompanied Napoleon as he had moved on to a stud in Normandy. However, according to an article by Louis

Merllié, published in 1980: 'in Vienna [Napoleon] was riding Coquet, another grey; at Moscow Ali whom he was already riding at Marengo.'

The shortage of water became so acute that the men fought over muddy holes; the Emperor himself had to be satisfied with liquid mud. Then even the mud dried up. Dust clouds rose as the men plodded along in their tight columns. Visibility for a while was retricted to only two feet. The eyes, ears and noses of both men and horses were full of dust – their faces were encrusted with it. Thirst caused men to fall on their bellies in the road and drink from puddles of horse urine. The famished animals ate withered grass so quickly that they swallowed stones caught in the roots and died.

In the first week of September Napoleon developed a high fever accompanied by a dry cough and extreme thirst. He was having difficulty in passing urine and what he did pass was dark and sedimented. He told his doctor: 'I am getting old, my legs are swelling, I hardly urinate.' These symptoms were to be recurring problems during the campaign and for the rest of his life. His poor health and lack of vigour were now noticeable.

On 7 September an auspicious sun rose bright and clear. 'It is the sun of Austerlitz,' said Napoleon. At five a.m. he jumped on to Lutzelberg, a German horse. They were seventy miles from Moscow and only 130,000 men had survived. The atrocious Battle of Borodino – known also as the Battle of Moskova – immortalised by Tolstoy, began with 103,000 French infantry and 30,600 cavalry. During that day Napoleon would ride two other horses, Emir and Courtois. Murat, in his bright self-designed uniform, fought like the devil. The fighting went on for twelve hours, until ten p.m. The ground, thick with dead and dying, was soon invaded by a wave of survivors, many of them women and children, who crawled over the battlefield to rescue anything of value. Blood-covered boots were snatched, as were clothes and any sustenance.

The day after the battle, the Emperor mounted Tauris and

contemplated the spectacle in front of him. His face was grim. The Russian losses were 44,000 men killed or wounded, including twenty-three generals, while the French losses were around 28,000. This narrow victory left the road ahead open.

'Peace lies in Moscow,' said Napoleon. 'When the great nobles of Russia see us masters of the capital, they will think twice about fighting on. If I liberated the serfs it would smash all those great fortunes. The battle will open the eyes of my brother Alexander, and the capture of Moscow will open the eyes of his nobles.' Napoleon's officers tried to dissuade him from going onwards. Murat warned: 'Moscow will destroy us.' Napoleon believed that as Alexander had made peace with him after Austerlitz and Friedland he would now make peace after the victory at Borodino.

On 14 September, in front of the Asiatic city of Moscow, Napoleon stood admiring the gilded cupolas of the churches and contemplated the River Moskva, 'unstained with blood since the Tartar invasions'. It had taken the army twelve weeks to reach the city Napoleon had planned to enter as the Tsar's brother-in-law. Like other places on the dreadful march, Moscow was defenceless and silent. The hooves of Napoleon's horse made a mournful sound in the empty streets. Most of the 300,000 inhabitants had fled, taking with them most, but not all, of the treasures, the arsenal, and personal and state property. Only about 1,500 locals witnessed the arrival of the French. Caulaincourt, who had strongly advised Napoleon against the Russian campaign, knew the people and the city well, for he had left his post as French Ambassador to Russia only a year earlier. (During his four years in Russia he had not forgotten his horses and had sent many dispatches about their care to France, including a touching one in 27 December 1808 giving instructions to retire Lachera, an old horse at Saint Cloud.)

At the crack of dawn after his first night in Moscow, Napoleon jumped on Emir and headed down what had been the busiest street in the city, the sound of hooves sharp and clear in the stillness. In the distance the French flag flew above the Kremlin where the Tsar's apartment stood empty. The clocks were still ticking and the freshly made bed was waiting for its rightful owner, who had gone to St Petersburg. Napoleon moved in, making the rooms his by hanging Gérard's portrait of his son on the wall.

Unbeknown to the French, the city of wooden houses was slowly breaking out into huge and terrible fires, which swept across suburbs, destroying hundreds of years of art and craftsmanship. Tchaikovsky's dramatic 1812 Overture, with the Marseillaise, the Tsarist national anthem, cathedral bells and cannon fire, evokes the engulfing flames that gave Russia its victory over Napoleon. Count Rostopchine, the Governor of Moscow, had released Russian prisoners and ordered them to start fires anywhere and everywhere, having first removed the hydrants which could have extinguished the inferno. Relentless flames roaring like huge waves engulfed the city.

At that point the French began to understand the utter desperation and determination of the Russians. They were burning their city rather than let it become the winter headquarters of the invaders; they would die rather than submit. Napoleon's position was now critical. The Kremlin was surrounded by fire. Trying to escape by crossing the little river around the complex, Napoleon and his suite, suffocating and blinded by smoke, became hopelessly lost. His faithful horse Tauris, led by an equerry, suddenly appeared through the smoke. Napoleon mounted him, found the St Petersburg Road and took refuge at the Petrovsk Palace, where he spent the rest of the night.

The next morning Napoleon rode back through the town to inspect the charred and blackened ruins. He was horrified. This proud and beautiful city of 1,600 steeples and more than 1,000 palaces was no more. Three houses out of every four were burnt down. The French rounded up 400 Russians who admitted to being incendiaries and shot them.

147

The French troops nearly choked on the foul smell of slow burning, but everyone devoured winter stores – food, wine and brandy. An immense stock of provisions had been found in Moscow's cellars and forage could be procured by sending detachments into the country and taking it from the peasants.

On 20 September, Napoleon, aware of Alexander's emotional instability, his indecision and his weak, effeminate character, sent an offer of peace: 'If Your Majesty still retains some part of your old feelings for me . . .' Napoleon had hoped to do so much with Alexander.

Napoleon wasted a month waiting for a response. Snow began to fall. Desperate, he sent emissary after emissary. Alexander ignored them, relying on 'General Winter' to defeat the French. The food for both men and animals in the cellars below the burnt-out city began to run out. Options were limited. Napoleon vacillated about whether to spend the winter in Moscow or to march to Germany. He feared that a long absence from home might jeopardise his position and that of his son. Once he had decided to leave, he sent an order for the purchase of more horses from Holstein and Jutland and demanded that the cavalry stock up for two months. This order was a further indication of the lack of judgement that was leading him to make catastrophic decisions which decimated his men and horses. What were these extra horses to eat en route? Paris was 1,600 miles away in a straight line. If they had waited for the spring, the men could have scythed off new grass for the animals, but the ground was still frozen.

Napoleon led the retreat, while Marshal Ney was in charge of the rearguard. The Russian army, meanwhile, was poised to encircle the French army on the vast plains and harass them until their defeat. The route back was teeming with soldiers and Cossacks – all eager to capture Napoleon and deliver him as a prisoner, a prize, to Alexander. Every short French man had to be extra vigilant in case he was mistaken for his Emperor.

11

Retreat from Moscow

*The seat on a horse makes gentlemen of some
and grooms of others.*

CERVANTES,
Don Quixote

On 19 October 1812, after thirty-five days in Moscow, the retreat of
the Grande Armée began. A long column of soldiers – many wrapped
up in sheepskin jackets and fur hats – mounted or on foot, slowly
trudged away from Moscow. They were forced to travel along the
same devastated track that they had wearily and hungrily followed in
the summer. Having squandered the cavalry in the advance to
Moscow, there were now only 15,000 of them left. Despite tremendous
losses, though, there were 90,000 to 100,000 infantry and 600 cannon.
Behind them came an encumbrance: thousands of civilians, French,
German and Russian, who had abandoned the burnt-out city. They
were domestics, retainers, wives, children, prostitutes, even actresses
from the Comédie-Française who had been working in Russia.

The draught horses were made to pull huge loads because
Napoleon refused to leave any artillery behind. 'The enemy would

make a trophy of it,' he explained. 'All will come with me.' Later, he added: 'One must be prepared to destroy everything so as not to leave any trophies to the enemy. I would prefer to eat with my fingers for the rest of the campaign rather than leave to the Russians a single fork with my crest.' Also in the crates of cargo was loot destined for Paris, including a giant gold cross from one of the churches. Gilded souvenirs were tucked in the men's knapsacks. The imperial equipage had 630 surviving horses. The remaining fifty-two wagons, drawn by exhausted horses, weary and underfed, were forced to travel fourteen or fifteen hours a day.

Chaotic scenes were now a daily occurrence. Keeping to the road prevented foraging by either horses or men. There was food in the wagons for only a couple of weeks at the most and hardly enough to last the horses a week. At every stop, and sometimes in between, drivers branched out through the countryside in the forlorn hope of discovering leftover food and fodder in the barren hamlets and deserted villages. Being uncertain what the next day would bring, they kept what they found carefully to themselves. Often they did not even have time to light a fire. The surgeons and doctors, without food, physic or bandages, and for the most part not even having bread for themselves, could not help the sick or wounded. The horses ate any straw within their reach – on roofs and out of beds – and tore the bark off trees, which caused digestive ailments and painful wind. They also suffered from lameness caused by lack of horseshoes.

Napoleon was unable to work out a strategy against the Cossacks' guerrilla tactics, unused to a war in which individuals and small groups acted on their own initiative. The same tactics were being employed by Viscount Wellesley (soon to become the Duke of Wellington) to defeat the French troops in Spain. Nor was there a solution to hunger. As soon as a horse fell, starving men would throw themselves on it, tearing open its side and grabbing the liver – the most tender piece. Caulincourt wrote:

Bad luck for the horse that fell! It was pounced on at once, and its driver could seldom protect it. The first-comers attacked the rump. The more expert cut open the flank and took the best morsel, the liver, which was, of course, the tenderest. While all this went on, no one ever thought to knock the poor beast in the head; everyone was too anxious to get back on the march.

The cold nights were too much for man and beast. In less than a week the weather had become so bad and the ground so sodden with rain that many of the draught horses were finished. But Napoleon kept riding. According to Caulaincourt:

By night or by day, the Emperor would mount his horse without warning: he even took pleasure in going out all of a sudden and throwing everyone off the scent. His saddle-horses were divided into troops. Each troop consisted of two horses for himself, one for the Master of Horse, and as many as were necessary for the other officers on duty with the Emperor. Throughout the whole twenty-four hours there was always one troop of horses saddled and bridled. Every officer had also to have a horse bridled; and the picket on duty, which consisted of an officer and twenty light horse, was always saddled and bridled. On the other campaigns there was one squadron in attendance, but on the Russian there were four – half light cavalry and half grenadiers and dragoons.

When the Emperor mounted his horse in the field he usually set out at a gallop, if only for two or three hundred yards. However keen and alert they were, therefore, it was difficult for a troop to be actually alongside him from the very start.

On 24 October the army had to change its route after discovering that the selected southern way was blocked by the Russians. Rather than force his way through, Napoleon decided reluctantly to return to

France the way he had come. He knew that that road, already churned up by heavy traffic and stripped of any provisions, would be a nightmare, but there was no other way. Already scarce when the men were going north, the food was now completely exhausted. Starving men strayed continuously from the columns in a desperate attempt to find something to eat, only to be slaughtered by the Cossacks.

The march was hard on the horses too and the pathetic remains of the cavalry were incapable of protecting everyone. The Cossacks were always in the background, unseen, but deadly as they harassed, killed and plundered. They appeared and disappeared like wolves. Dressed in uniforms, especially the headgear and jackets, looted from murdered soldiers, they were difficult to distinguish from the ragged French army.

On 27 October, when the snow started in earnest, the real horror of the retreat began. Horses and men stumbled through the snow. Tolstoy later described their pitiable appearance: 'disfigured by frost-bitten cheeks and noses, and almost all of them had red, swollen and streaming eyes.' The snow was not yet thick enough to prevent crows and ravens from picking at the last decomposing human and horse remains strewn over vast distances in Borodino where, just seven weeks earlier, the terrible battle had taken place.

The cold was so intense that men could hardly hold the reins. The shortage of horseshoes was now acute. Most horses could not cope with the weather conditions, so some troopers tied sacks around their animals' feet to stop them slipping on ice. Napoleon was pleased with Roitelet because he did not slip like many of the other horses.

After Borodino the severe cold made roads impassable. In the next week over 30,000 horses died. Parts of the baggage train and artillery broke down and were abandoned. Men continued to desert by night to find shelter and, as there was no cavalry left to protect them, thousands fell into the hands of the hidden Cossacks. When they reached Smolensk the Russians came out in full force, appearing as if from nowhere. Two armies were converging to attack, one army from the north, another from the south. But there was no clash. When, on 14 November, the French army left Smolensk, Napoleon walked, leaning on a birch stick, with the cavalry and with the Guard. Walking was the only way to fight the cold. Then horrendous news arrived: the Russians had burnt the bridge at Borissov, trapping them on the vast plains.

Hunger was prevalent. Larrey, the surgeon, told of having seen a captain's wife, dressed in a sable coat, eating the flesh of a horse which had just fallen. Its belly had been opened and having no knife, she put her head straight into its entrails.

A week later there was a glimmer of hope as the always popular Ney, thought to have been lost with the rearguard, managed to rejoin the Emperor. Napoleon, the master of Europe, had become little more than a general retreating through a hostile country. His chances of being captured were high. Wolves, too, suddenly appeared through the woods. The terrible route from Moscow was littered with bodies – even the skeletons of horses between the shafts of coaches – and abandoned belongings.

The temperature oscillated between minus 21 and minus 31 degrees and the men had to camp in the open air. Every day famine, disease, frost and snow decimated the survivors, many of whom were now barefoot. Stragglers were finished off by the ever-present Cossacks. Men lost ears, noses and toes in the cold. Their frozen hair and beards tinkled as they marched through the blizzards. Of the huge caravan that left Moscow, there remained only the Emperor's *calèche* and about twenty other vehicles.

On 24 November Napoleon reached the Beresina River with just 26,000 to 30,000 soldiers, weak with hunger and cold, plus 40,000 sick, wounded and hangers on. The French were no longer a threat to the 120,000-strong Russian combat forces ready to face them. Napoleon was lost unless he could get himself and his men quickly over the river, their only escape route.

153

The cold had been less severe for a few days, but that temporary thaw had swollen the river and made fording it impossible. Three Russian armies, outnumbering the French by almost four to one, were converging for the final kill and to capture Napoleon. Trapped, he was determined not to be forced to surrender unconditionally while on Russian soil.

A place had to be found to ford the river; an area shallow enough to build a temporary pontoon. And fast. Meanwhile, the general who had found the town of Borissov occupied by the Russians now saw a Lithuanian peasant whose horse was wet through to his collar. Realising that the horse must have crossed the river, he forced the peasant to show him where this was possible. The passage to freedom was approximately nine miles above Borissov, in front of the village of Studianka.

On 25 November, under Napoleon's supervision, his men started building a pontoon. Luckily, two of the forges were still part of the caravan and there was enough charcoal to weld metal into shape. Despite the freezing conditions – the river was carrying blocks of ice – 400 men, completely naked and waist-deep in water, started building across the river at the ford. Napoleon was there urging the men on, handing them wine to keep them going. Every minute the Russians were getting closer. Piles were driven into the mud, joists were bolted and planks from nearby demolished houses arranged across them. Then an additional, heavier bridge was built to take the horses, wagons and artillery. As a decoy to mislead the Russians, another group of men chopped trees further away. What was left of the Grande Armée, with their swollen joints and ragged uniforms, started to cross. They were led by Napoleon riding Tauris, whose speed and foresight had earlier saved him from a Cossack ambush. However, the Russians started firing on the thousands limping over the structure, and more than 10,000 stragglers stayed on the Russian side of the bridge after its destruction only to be annihilated.

Among the last people and horses to reach the pontoon was the widow of a colonel, killed only a few days earlier. One of the minority fortunate enough still to have a horse, she held in her arms her most precious possession, her four-year-old daughter. In a few minutes her horse was shot and soon a bullet shattered her thigh. With despair in her eyes she fiercely cuddled the crying child, kissed her several times and, taking the blood-soaked garter from her wounded leg, strangled her. This done, she slumped down beside her dying horse and, holding her child tight against her heart, waited for death. Soon all three were trampled by the panic-stricken horses pressing on to the bridge under fire from the Russians.

On 3 December Napoleon issued a public statement, the twenty-ninth of the *Bulletins de la Grande Armée*, in which he confessed that an atrocious calamity had befallen his army and that the Russian campaign had ended in disaster. This was in contrast to the usual tone of his bulletins in which, always mindful of the value of favourable publicity, he spoke directly to his subjects giving them an official version of events designed to boost public morale; defeats were usually attributed to inferiority of numbers. Local prefects posted the bulletins at town halls throughout France and they were also published in the official newspaper, the *Moniteur*. Napoleon believed that through the bulletins, ordinary soldiers and civilians could feel that they were in contact with the destiny of France. The bulletin recorded that, after leaving Smolensk,

> the horses of the cavalry, of the artillery, and of the wagons, perished every night, not by hundreds, but by thousands – especially the French and German horses; above 30,000 horses died in a few days; our cavalry was all dismounted; our artillery and our wagons were without the means of transport; we were obliged to abandon and destroy a large part of our cannon, and our munitions of war and provisions.

155

*Napoleon's campaign in France, painted by Ernest Meissonier
(1815–1891) many years after the event.*

Anticipating the alarm that this news would cause in France, Napoleon
decided to leave his army and return to Paris. He needed to exchange
the role of fugitive at the head of a dying army for that of master of
Europe once again; he had heard of a conspiracy to overthrow him;
he wanted to return to Paris to quell rumours of his death; he knew,
too, that Viscount Wellesley had won the Battle of Salamanca in Spain
and was strengthening the British position against France.

On 5 December Napoleon and Caulaincourt took the road west.
The carriage was too heavy for the snowed-up road and the horses
slipped and struggled on the ice. On reaching Kowno, Caulaincourt
discovered a shabby covered red sledge. Abandoning Roustam and
the luggage, including Napoleon's dressing case, they transferred to
it. Day and night, travelling incognito, they swished through the snow,
cutting across East Prussia and into Poland – leaving the corpses and

ghosts of the army far behind. The postilions lashed at the straining horses and the red box slid and lurched through the snow. In Dresden on 13 December they continued to Paris in a carriage lent by the King of Saxony. On 18 December Napoleon surprised his sleeping wife at the Tuileries.

In the last days of 1812 the disorganised remnants of the Grande Armée staggered across the Niemen into East Prussia, where they were mocked. The sight of the once invincible army limping back in rags from Russia gave the youth of Germany the confidence to be openly hostile to Napoleon. Agitated and excited, they received the splinters of the broken army with derision and delight. There was great joy at the sight of their suffering, because it showed that Napoleon was no longer all-conquering. What had hitherto been a secret underground movement in Germany now broke out into open resistance. Schoolboys danced around the men in the streets, yelling insulting songs. In the rest of Europe and in France the catastrophe stirred people to defy Napoleon: when news that he had suffered a defeat reached England, guns were fired from the Tower of London in celebration; anti-French feeling was exploited by Prussia; Austria also adopted a hostile attitude and withdrew troops; and in Paris political affairs were more than agitated. People began to count the cost of Napoleon's Empire.

The Russian campaign had consumed the largest number of men and horses of any of the Napoleonic wars. Unlike other battles, where most of the losses took place on the field of battle, most of these deaths, both of horses and humans, were caused by malnutrition, hypothermia and exhaustion. About 60,000 men, at the most, returned. It is difficult to estimate the full extent of the disaster, but according to one Russian report the dead from both sides totalled 430,707 men and 230,677 animals, mostly horses. The horses of the Guard fared better than most. Out of 4,000 animals, 773 survived. We know also that Leonore, Roitelet, Embelli, Emir, Tauris and

Courtois went to Moscow and back. But was Marengo one of the horses who went as part of Napoleon's moving stables? Vincent Cronin, the English biographer, wrote in his best-selling *Napoleon*, that Marengo was, indeed, the horse whom Napoleon often rode when on the long road to Moscow, but the records show no horse with this name. Yet Marengo, when on display in London in 1823, was wearing the superb saddle and bridle he wore in Moscow and his months with Napoleon in Russia were always included in summaries of his long career.

12

The End of the Empire

To all Grey Horses! Fill up again
For the sake of a grey horse dear to me;
For a foam-fed bit and a snatching rein
And a reaching galloper fast and free!
To all Grey Horses! For one steed's sake

W. H. Ogilvie,
'Fair Girls and Grey Horses' (1913)

Britain, Prussia, Austria and Russia now formed the another coalition against France. Even Napoleon's father-in-law, Francis, was fighting against him. Napoleon could not, of course, replace the troops or horses lost in Russia; so short was manpower that young conscripts were trained in the use of muskets and bayonets while marching to battle. Napoleon was heavily hampered by the lack of cavalry, as the French were unable to pursue fleeing adversaries and finalise their victories. While conscription could bring more men, nothing could replace the tens of thousands of horses lost in Russia. This letter from Napoleon, dated 7 March 1813, shows how he acquired horses from unlikely places:

159

The Cavalry must be dealt with under four heads: men, horses, saddles and harness, and accoutrements . . . Of the *horses* there are three categories. An agreement has been made for the purchase of 4,000 – has it been executed? Find out their distribution amongst the regiments. 15,000 are to come from the Departments; find out by which Department each regiment is to be provided, also the places and the depots to which these horses are to come. The same applies to the 16,000 given by the towns and cantons. Besides these there have been 3,200 horses promised by individuals; where and how are they being allocated? These four categories make up an aggregate of 3,800 horses, which with the addition of those at the depots gives a total of over 40,000.

In the desperate year of 1813 twenty-three portraits of Napoleon's horses were ordered. Marengo does not appear in any of these, nor does he appear on the Registers at this stage, let alone in those paintings of horses reproduced by the porcelain factory at Sèvres for ceremonial dinner plates. If Marengo had been that important then surely his portrait would have been painted. Then again, the Registers were not always thorough. Although both Lowka and Calvados were singled out for painting, neither appears in them.

Horace Vernet was commissioned and paid 250 francs each for ten portraits: Vizir, Gisors, Lowka, Favori, Harbet, Neron, Wagram, Calvados, Tamerlan (who seems to have been a different horse from the earlier Tamerlan in Egypt) and Hippogriffe. Alexandre-Ivanovich Sauerwied painted Curde, Labrador, Cirus, Cid, Cordoue, Sara, Sagonte, Epicurien, Intendant, Embelli, Gessner, Breant and Wurtzbourg. Ali was not chosen to be painted as he had already left the imperial stables. He had been drawn earlier in 1809 and in 1812 Horace Vernet had painted his portrait. By now there was an added confusion about Ali's name. At the end of 1810 Roustam the

Mameluke was given a young French assistant, Louis Saint-Denis, who adopted an oriental style of dress and called himself 'Ali'.

Perhaps Napoleon had the portraits painted as a positive act in what was a dismal situation. Not only was he surrounded by enemies at home, but the French armies in Spain were being forced to retreat by Wellesley, who had become known as the Liberador de España. Napoleon had some successes in Saxony and Lusatia (later part of Prussia) against the Russians and the Prussians, but his army was torn to shreds at Leipzig at the 'Battle of the Nations' in October 1813 – his worst defeat – and he was forced to retreat over the Rhine. At the battles of Dresden, Leipzig and Hanau and in the last battles of 1814, Napoleon rode his faithful little Tauris. Murat withdrew to Naples, never to return to the command of the French cavalry.

In late 1813 Napoleon was fighting on French soil for the first time. Over 600,000 Russians, Austrians and Prussians marched on Paris from the north and the east, while Wellesley was advancing from the south. Napoleon was fighting against seven powers: Bavaria, Britain, Prussia, Russia, Saxony, Sweden and Austria. During this campaign his slapdash riding techniques came in for further criticism. No censure was more severe than in Ernst Otto Odeleben's *Relation circonstanciée de la campagne de Saxe en 1813*:

Napoleon rode like a butcher. He held the bridle in his right hand, with the left arm pendent. He looked as though he were suspended on his saddle. Whilst galloping, his body rolled backwards and forwards and sideways, according to the speed of his horse. As soon as the animal stepped aside, its rider lost his seat, and as we know Napoleon more than once was thrown.

On 9 November the Allies offered peace if the borders of France were reduced to the natural frontiers of the Rhine, the Alps and the Pyrenees. Napoleon refused. With just 50,000 men he continued with whirlwind tactics to win victory after victory, one of them in the fields around his old school at Brienne.

The three-year-old King of Rome and Marie Louise were obliged to take refuge in Austria. Napoleon was only as far away as Fontaine-bleau when he heard the news that Paris had capitulated. On 1 April, for the first time since the fifteenth century, a foreign army marched through the streets of the French capital. The Allies entered Paris led by Tsar Alexander, the King of Prussia, and Prince Schwarzenberg who represented Austria. Napoleon's marshals explained that his troops, worn and demoralised, could hold out no longer.

Ney advised the Emperor to abdicate, which he did on 6 April when he heard that a whole army corps had gone over to the enemy. He agreed to be exiled to the little Mediterranean island of Elba. He was allowed to take with him a large number of his Guard and some of his favourite horses; but even at this stage there is no mention of a horse called Marengo in the archives among the horses either accompanying him to Elba or left with other favourite Arabs, such as Austerlitz and Marie, in the Tuileries stables.

Since 1808 Napoleon had carried with him a satchel containing a dose of poison. In 1812 he had changed this for another mixture. This new preparation failed him on the night of 12 April when, desperate and confused, he decided to end his life. That night, after his attempted suicide, he confessed to Caulaincourt: 'I anticipate that they are going to separate me from the Empress and my son – they are going to bestow on me all kind of humiliations. They will try to assassinate me, or at least to insult me [which] would be far worse than death.'

The sadness of Napoleon's farewell to the soldiers of the Old Guard, many of them veterans of Austerlitz and Jena, was captured in the painting *Les Adieux de Fontainebleau*. To broken-hearted cries of '*Vive l'Empereur!*', on 20 April Napoleon descended the monumental double horseshoe staircase of Fontainebleau to start his journey to exile. The Old Guard were waiting for him in the palace courtyard, then known as La Cour du Cheval Blanc (from a statue of Marcus Aurelius on a white horse which stood in its centre) and later renamed La Cour des Adieux in honour of this poignant moment. Napoleon responded by embracing their flags and then made his much-repeated speech:

> Soldiers of my old guard, I take leave of you. For twenty years I have seen you always upon the path of honour and glory. During the last few weeks, you have been models of bravery and fidelity, just as in the years of good fortune . . . But there could have been civil war. That is why I sacrificed all other interests to those of the country. I am going away.

Leaving La Cour du Cheval Blanc behind, Napoleon, followed by his large household and Sir Neil Campbell, the English Commissioner, took the lonely road to Elba. He would still be Emperor – albeit of a tiny kingdom – and with the annoying presence of English troops to ensure that he did not return to the Continent. During the journey he was nearly lynched by a mob of Royalists in Provence. The anger of a people exhausted by his conscriptions, wars and the effects of his continental system pursued him as he travelled south. This opposition caused him, at one stage, to change his clothes and travel incognito.

The new King Louis XVIII did not rush to take the empty throne in Paris. He was late leaving England because of yet another severe attack of gout. Fifty-eight, enormously fat, with painful feet which he kept in cushion-like containers, he could walk only with someone on either side to support him. After the Prince Regent had bidden him farewell, he set off to reclaim the kingdom lost by his brother, Louis XVI, twenty-one years earlier. By chance he set foot in Paris on 4 May, the same day that Napoleon landed on Elba. The 'joyous entry' into the capital of the man known in England as 'Bungy Louis', in buttoned Prussian trousers and a British naval coat, was made in a barouche drawn by eight pale horses from the imperial stables, attended by grooms wearing the Emperor's livery and accompanied by the Imperial Guard. At the gate of St Denis, after receiving the keys of Paris, he proceeded to the home of his ancestors, the Tuileries.

Relying on wheels and heavy padding for his transport, Louis XVIII, unlike his two brothers, was no horseman, but he now had the final word on what happened in both the stables and studs. There were few changes in the stables at the Tuileries, and it seems that many of Napoleon's horses remained there. They were not ridden by the new King who was far too fat to mount – unless he was hoisted on to the saddle. It is difficult to find words to describe the revulsion he elicited in those who met him: 'his pottle belly Majesty', 'the Sir John Falstaff of France', 'Louis Dix Huitres' (a pun on his passion for oysters); men playing cards would shout 'pig of clubs' or 'pig of diamonds'. Later, even Wellington was not shy about expressing his opinion of the obese monarch: 'I had a very bad opinion of Louis XVIII – he was selfish and false to the highest degree.' He also said that '[Louis] was a walking sore – not a part of him was sound'. Some people, though, found him witty, even wise. Louis' reign was to be plagued both by reactionaries among the returned émigrés and by his own ill-health. He had only one asset: he was the legitimate heir to the throne of France. Much in France remained the same under the restored monarchy. Even Talleyrand stayed in power and the Banque de France was untouched. In the stables Rieussel, too, made the transition from the reign of Napoleon to that of Louis. And so did the horses.

Members of English society, especially the Roman Catholic aristocracy, who had helped Louis and his court during their long exile in England, now rushed to Paris to see him in the Tuileries, instead of Hartwell House in Hertfordshire. Even those who were not invited to receptions were free to go to the church services at the

Tuileries, where the music was excellent. Among the frequent English visitors to those services were Captain Henry Howard, who was later to play such a part in Marengo's career in England. Closely related to the Duke of Norfolk's family and educated at Strasbourg, he was one of the many Roman Catholics who had supported the French Royal Family during their exile in England. Now aged fifty-seven, he travelled with his second wife Catherine, thirteen years his junior, and their three children. Although in her memoirs Mrs Howard related paying a formal call on the newly created Duke of Wellington in Paris, she does not mention being presented at Court to the new King who received ladies once or twice a week. (The ladies had to wait in the salon of Diana for Louis to be wheeled into the throne room, for he could hardly walk.) She did write, though, that she perceived 'a rooted aversion to the English, in the lower classes, which perhaps is kept up by the presence of their conqueror, the Duke of Wellington, who strikes awe'.

One of the first tasks for the restored Bourbons was to rid the palaces of the thousands of decorative Bonaparte bees which filled the rooms. An army of ladies of the Court worked rapidly to unpick them from the yards of sumptuous silk and velvet hangings. Others simply embroidered patches of fleur-de-lis over the bees as the King, his painful feet encased in his huge slippers, ambled from palace to palace. The letters N and B were removed from furniture. Violets, too, were outlawed – being seen as a flower of subversion, a sign of rebellion. They had become too strongly associated with Napoleon. Shop signs with violets were placed out of view. Difficult, if not impossible, to erase and replace, however, were the Napoleonic crests branded on the rump of the Emperor's personal horses.

Continual wars had kept the British out of the continent since the end of the Peace of Amiens eleven years earlier. Now, yet again, they could and did flock to Paris, to Rome, to Florence – and to the pretty little city of Brussels, where everything was so much more affordable than in London. Among the more settled visitors to Paris was Wellington, who had been educated at a French school in Ireland and had finished his education on the continent. Having overthrown the French in Portugal and driven Joseph Bonaparte from the Spanish throne, he was posted to Paris as British Ambassador. Continuing his conquests in peacetime, he had become the lover of one of Napoleon's former mistresses, Josephine Weimer, a formidable actress known on the stage as Mademoiselle Georges – a portrait of whom he kept in his private sitting room, together with another of Napoleon's most infamous sister, Pauline. A friendship with Madame Grassini was also rumoured. Wellington's takeover was complete when he arranged for the purchase of Pauline Bonaparte's magnificent mansion (which is still the British Embassy) complete with furniture. So Wellington, the man who would defeat the Emperor, was sleeping in a Bonaparte bed in the house which loyal Pauline had sold to help her dethroned brother.

13

Elba and the Hundred Days

They say princes learn no art truly but the art of
horsemanship. The reason is the brave beast is no
flatterer. He will throw a prince as soon as his
groom.

BEN JONSON,
Discoveries

Pauline arrived on Elba at the end of October and found Napoleon
established in an unimpressive but pretty palace above the sea,
surrounded by his usual officials and staff, including chefs, two
equerries, two valets and eight footmen. His longing for company,
particularly that of his son, was intense, his loneliness acute. Pauline
stayed for four months, the only one of his siblings ever to join him in
exile. Josephine had died at Malmaison at the end of May and now
Marie Louise's repeated and flimsy excuses made it abundantly clear
that she would never set foot on Elba. Still he hoped to see her, even
though he knew that Count Neipperg, a general in the Austrian army,
had already become her lover. (She had two children by him during
Napoleon's lifetime and married him as soon as she became a widow.)

Even then horses remained a vital part of Napoleon's life and thirty-five men worked in the Salt Warehouse which housed them and his twenty-seven carriages, the most elaborate of which was the sleeper which had brought him from Fontainebleau. The seats could be turned into beds and a cooking stand brought into use. These were the responsibility of Vincent, the head saddler. Apart from Napoleon's personal horses there were forty-eight carriage horses. Among his top favourites were Wagram, Tauris, Roitelet and Intendant. There were also at least two horses that had been used in Spain but had not featured in other European battles: Emir, a Turk, with thick black mane and tail; and Gonsalve, a big Spanish bay with flowing mane and tail, also ridden by Napoleon in 1814 at Brienne. The remaining Arab horses were Heliopolis and Euphrates, who were given to his aides. At Lützen, when Napoleon was riding Roitelet, a bullet shot off some of the horse's hair, which never grew back. When Napoleon visited the stables he would look at the scar and give the horse a lump of sugar, saying: 'Eh, we escaped nicely that time, both of us.'

Although Napoleon organised the island as if it were an empire and introduced many reforms and improvements, he finally had time for leisure: he sometimes swam on the beach below his little palace, he gardened a little, he spent time with his horses and, liberated from the pressure of work, he rode to his heart's content. But it is absolutely certain that no little grey Arab by the name of Marengo was in his stables at that time.

Under the Treaty of Fontainebleau Napoleon should have received two million francs a year from Louis XVIII, but this was not paid. The four million francs which Napoleon had brought with him had gone, paying for the 600-strong Imperial Guard and his large court. His dire financial position, coupled with reports that the Bourbon government was planning to remove him to the Azores, the West Indies or St Helena, and that Louis XVIII had approved a report recommending the confiscation of all Bonaparte property in France, provoked him to leave. The final impetus was given by newspaper articles sent to him by Lady Holland from Florence, where she was then staying. In one of these, *The Courier*, he read of the allied sovereigns' plan to exile him to a more remote destination.

Napoleon – with a diamond necklace given to him by Pauline in his luggage – his officers and troops, left Elba on 26 February 1815. The horses on board included Gonsalve, Tauris, Roitelet and Wagram. Major I. H. Vivian, who interviewed Napoleon on Elba six weeks before his departure, later wrote that while Napoleon may have planned to flee, the timing was not premeditated. 'An opinion prevailed on the Continent, immediately after the escape of Bonaparte from Elba, that the British Government had connived at his departure; and in England I have heard that Colonel Campbell was censured for not having exercised a proper degree of vigilance.' By chance Napoleon arrived at Golfe Juan near Antibes on 1 March. This fulfilled a prediction made by many soldiers when he went into exile that he would return when the violets next bloomed. The violet became a rallying sign for his supporters during the Restoration: '*Vive le Père la Violette!*' his followers shouted, while women waved bunches of the flower at him. On the road to Grenoble he was enthusiastically received by the soldiers who were sent to stop his progress. In Lyons he issued a series of decrees: the badges of the Bourbons should be destroyed and replaced by the emblems of the Empire; the law which had restored the unsold estates was annulled; and the feudal titles which Louis had revived were abolished, as were the Swiss Guard.

Newspaper headlines in England marked his progress: 'Most Important News. Landing of Bonaparte in France.' This was followed ten days later by: 'Widespread Desertion of Troops to Bonaparte.' And on 23 March: 'Departure of Louis XVIII from Paris. Arrival of Bonaparte.' As Major Vivian wrote: 'The extraordinary and rapid march to Paris, without the loss of a single life, was a circumstance so completely beyond all calculation, as to afford a decisive proof of the enthusiasm which so generally existed throughout France, in favour of Bonaparte.' He went on to explain how such eagerness could not be created by any plot. Napoleon's return was successful because of the ardour of the people.

Marshal Ney, who had gone over to Louis XVIII's side, was sent to arrest Napoleon, promising to bring him to the King 'in an iron cage'. Instead, caught up in the emotion which surrounded Napoleon, combined perhaps with the fact that he could not rely on his own troops, he offered his sword and his service to his old master. He told his men: 'The cause of the Bourbons is lost for ever.' Napoleon and Ney pushed rapidly onwards in the direction of Paris. The news of Ney's defection and their triumphal march so frightened Louis XVIII that on 19 March he climbed into his carriage and fled to Lille. So hasty was his departure that he left behind his old slippers, something he regretted bitterly as they had taken the shape of his feet. In Paris royal white cockades were tied to dogs' tails as an expression of contempt for its King.

The evening after Louis' coach left Paris, another carrying Napoleon accompanied by Caulaincourt, his former Master of the Horse, and surrounded by excited soldiers and an escort of Lancers, passed through quiet streets. It was 20 March – the third birthday of the King of Rome. Although the army thronged around Napoleon, the occupants in most houses stayed indoors, cautious or indifferent, and he arrived in the wet, cold early evening more or less incognito. People shrank from the idea of further war, conscription and the consequences of the continental blockade. Amidst flaring torches and waving caps the soldiers carried him shoulder-high through the doors of the Tuileries, up the grand staircase into the royal chambers. Once again he was hailed as Emperor. The white flag of the Bourbons was lowered and the tricolour raised on the flagstaff. Without firing a shot, Napoleon had regained his throne. Relays of fast horses criss-crossed Europe with daily bulletins of his progress. In Vienna, where kings and politicians were still working out Europe's balance of power, there was alarm, followed by amazement that any man could have inspired so strong an attachment.

Forming a new government was not difficult because most of Napoleon's former ministers returned. Three days after his entry into Paris, on 23 March, he sent instructions about his possessions in Elba:

> Recover from Elba any of my things that are worth sending. I am anxious to have my Corsican horse, if it is not ill, and can be sent back. The canary travelling-carriage, the big carriage, and two of the state coaches, are worth the trouble of returning as well as my underwear. I am presenting my library to the town, along with my house; the house will do for a casino, but the library must be left in it.

The reference to the Corsican horse is yet another stable mystery. It did not, of course, arrive in time for Waterloo, but other old favourites and new mounts were rounded up for Napoleon's use. Désirée and Marie, who had remained in the imperial stables when they reverted to being royal stables, were joined by newcomers. As Napoleon was determined to get as many horses as he could lay his hands on, it seems likely that Ali was returned from the studs at Le Pin and Angers, together with other Arabs. According to Napoleon's valet Constant: 'In the last few years of his reign [the Emperor] rode no other horses than Arabs. There were a few of these noble animals which the Emperor held in great affection.'

Even politicians who had been horrified by Napoleon's return gave him limited support because they thought it better to let him reign in peace, so France would present a firm front. But the fear of invasion led to fierce criticism; since his presence was the sole cause of the inevitable war it was felt that he should sacrifice himself and step down. In the palace a slackening in his flair and energy could be seen:

he slept more heavily and longer, he was slower. Even his brother Lucien advised him to abdicate in favour of his son. Newspapers discussed the question of abdication openly. Marie Louise showed no sign of returning, so there was little chance that her father would support him. As a compromise, Napoleon's faithful stepdaughter, Hortense, whose lover was one of his aides-de-camp, acted as his hostess.

Politically, matters were going badly for Napoleon, but it was a different story with his army. Attempts to reintroduce conscription failed, yet 15,000 volunteers enlisted and 25,000 retired soldiers rejoined. Missing, however, was his Minister of War, Louis Berthier, who had defected to Louis. Murat, an old friend, was told by Napoleon to stay away.

As usual, Napoleon seemed to pull horses out of the sky. While requisitioning half the horses from the *gendarmerie*, he also reclaimed 5,000 that had been lent to farmers and purchased over 6,000 more. So many thousands of horses were rounded up that, in early May, Wellington, apparently ignorant of the rift with Murat, wrote to Lord Uxbridge: 'I have a most formidable account of the French cavalry. They have now 16,000 grosse cavalerie, of which 6,000 are cuirassiers. They are getting horses to mount 42,000 cavalry, heavy and light. It is reported that Murat has fled from Italy by sea . . . He will probably command them.' (Uxbridge later commanded Wellington's cavalry at Waterloo, where he lost a leg.)

While inside France it was made clear to Napoleon that he needed to introduce more liberal ideas and reform the constitution, outside France all the states of Christian Europe had declared war on him – they would fight until his capture, defeat or death. In Vienna the plenipotentiaries of Europe's eight leading powers declared him an outlaw. The four principal powers at the Congress of Vienna sat around a polished table and, despite their differences and quarrels – the Tsar was being grasping – signed a treaty against France. Each nation would supply 150,000 men. Other countries would send troops as well. The total would be a massive and invincible force of nearly one million soldiers. The English wanted to strike quickly.

Wellington, as head of the Anglo-Dutch-German army, moved to the Belgian capital Brussels, while seventy-four-year-old Prussian Commander, General Blücher, made his headquarters in the ancient city of Liège. Just as Kutuzov during the Russian campaign had taken revenge on Napoleon for his defeat at Austerlitz, Blücher would now even his own score with Napoleon.

14

Copenhagen

Boot, saddle, to horse, and away!

ROBERT BROWNING,
'Boot and Saddle'

On the afternoon of Wednesday 14 June 1815 – fifteen years after the Battle of Marengo – Napoleon's army, led by his magnificent cavalry, were advancing fast. They had crossed the border the night before and were heading for Brussels, racing to get there before reinforcements arrived to swell the British and Prussian armies. Speed was of the essence. Napoleon knew that he was outnumbered two to one. By driving a wedge between Wellington and Blücher and fighting them one at a time, he could still win. The Duke of Wellington was the one great general whom Napoleon had never beaten. Wellington, though, had a more generous appreciation of Napoleon, than Napoleon had of him.

When Wellington heard of the impending invasion he told the Duchess of Richmond – the beautiful and amusing Charlotte – not to cancel the ball which they had been planning for weeks, the preparations continued. The excitement of the London Season stretched across the Channel to Brussels. Wellington had sent out invitations for yet another ball the following Wednesday in his house at rue Royale. Many British army officers were accompanied by their wives and unmarried daughters, all of whom were enjoying Belgium's low cost of living and were determined to put on a confident front so as not to alarm the local population.

Napoleon and his men were rushing to push Wellington out of Brussels and prevent him from gathering sufficient strength to invade France. Napoleon would use the same tactic as he had at Ulm, Austerlitz, Jena and Friedland – attack at the earliest possible opportunity and maintain an offensive attitude. He would strike quickly before the arrival of Allied reinforcements. The Russians, he knew, could not get to Brussels until early July, another two weeks away. In that pre-railway era, armies relied on shoe leather.

As Napoleon's men marched towards Brussels, on 15 June the British officers' horses remained in readiness outside the Duchess of Richmond's house in rue de la Blanchisserie. While the English and Scots danced quadrilles in circles of light thrown by the crystal chandeliers under draped ceilings in the long, narrow room, the officers in their dazzling dress uniforms with epaulettes, frills of lace and embroidery, tried to ignore the looming battle. But the reveille was expected at any moment.

The ball was actually held in a former coachbuilder's depot across a courtyard from the Duchess's house. It lacked the splendour implied by Byron's verse in *Childe Harold* or by Thackeray in *Vanity Fair*. Byron's 'high hall' was only 13 feet high, while the room itself, although large, was only 120 feet long by 54 feet wide – and there were only 233 guests, not a thousand. But Byron still captured the atmosphere of that memorable evening:

> *There was a sound of revelry by night,*
> *And Belgium's capital had gather'd then*

Her beauty and her Chivalry, and bright
The lamps shone o'er fair women and brave men;
A thousand hearts beat happily; and when
Music arose with its voluptuous swell,
Soft eyes look'd love to eyes which spake again,
And all went merry as a marriage bell;
But hush! Hark! A deep sound strikes like a rising knell!

Not all the guests stayed, but most were there to applaud the Sergeants of the Gordon Highlanders in their green, red and blue tartan kilts after they gave a spirited display of Highland dancing. Despite the ostensible gaiety, the tension was apparent. Just before supper the arrival of Lieutenant Henry Webster from Quatre-Bras, making his way speedily across the dance floor in a muddy uniform with a message from the Prince of Orange, was almost a relief. Breathless with fright and excitement, he said that Napoleon was twenty miles away from Brussels at Quatre-Bras, where he had repulsed the Prussian forces. The roads at Mons were clear. The French concentration was at Charleroi. Nearby at Le Caillou, attached to a farmhouse on the Genappe road, was Napoleon's headquarters. In the stables were Napoleon's grand coach and some of his special horses, including Marie, Désirée and – according to many accounts – Marengo.

Wellington sat on a sofa chatting to Lady Hamilton Dalrymple, but they were constantly interrupted by his need to give instructions – even in the middle of a sentence he would call an officer over to issue an order. Minutes before supper the Iron Duke realised that Napoleon had fooled him. He had split him from his ally Blücher. The dancing stopped and the whispering grew louder as Wellington asked his host for a good map. The two Dukes entered the library. Then Wellington remarked: 'Napoleon has *humbugged* me, by God! He has gained twenty-four hours' march on me.' Immediately before supper the Duke of Brunswick and the Prince of Orange left. Wellington stayed on.

One by one officers were leaving, changing their buckled black patent leather dancing pumps and fine silk stockings for fighting boots. As they mounted their horses, Wellington explained: 'I have ordered the army to concentrate at Quatre-Bras; but we shall not stop there, and if so, I must fight him *here*,' letting his thumb rest on the map beyond the village of Waterloo. Most of the tempting food was left uneaten, brandy bottles remained unopened. The women's smiles faded as they, too, in their fashionable dresses and magnificent jewellery, faced their fear. No one dared think that shouts of '*Vive l'Empereur!*' might, within twenty-four hours, resound through that very room.

Wellington himself did not leave immediately. The crowd started to thin out as the men left to rejoin their regiments. Farewells were brisk and there was a feeling of confusion as the sound of bugles, raised voices and drums outside filtered through the ballroom. The rumour went around that Napoleon was almost at the gates of Brussels.

Unbeknown to them, the men were preparing for the last great battle to rely on the strength of massed cavalry. Wellington knew that even with its unspeakable loss of horses in Russia, the French cavalry was superior to the British. Its high standard was one of the French Empire's achievements. In the twenty-five years since the Revolution, promotion in the French army had been solely on merit. In Britain, any commission could be sold, whether captain, major or lieutenant-colonel. Many men, like Wellington or Viscount Combermere, matched their rank, but many others did not. The British cavalry was handicapped by lack of professional knowledge and experience among its wealthy officers, many of whom lacked professional ambition – or training. They still behaved on the battlefield as though they were riding to hounds. In Spain in 1808 the 20th Light Dragoons went badly out of control at Vimiero, as did the 23rd at Talavera the following year. On one occasion Wellington wrote of a trick our officers of cavalry have acquired of galloping at every thing, and then galloping back as fast as they gallop on the enemy. They never . . . think of manoeuvring before an enemy – so little that one would think they cannot manoeuvre, excepting on Wimbledon Common; and when they use their arm as it ought to be, viz offensively, they never keep . . . a reserve.

Napoleon also criticised the English cavalry. In his book on Napoleon, Barry O'Meara later summed up his comments:

Napoleon observed that he did not consider the English cavalry by any means equal to the infantry. The men, by some fault, were not able to stop the horses, and were liable to be cut to pieces, if, in the act of charging, it became necessary to halt and retreat. The horses too were accustomed to be fed too luxuriously, kept too warm, and from what he had learned, greatly neglected by the riders.

To the fading sound of the orchestra from the emptying ballroom, and with the blackness of the night broken by blazing torches, the British and Allied troops, officers and horses assembled. Some of the muskets' muzzles – Wellington's good sturdy 'Brown Bess' muskets – had candles stuck in them. Over the sound of fifes, bugles, bagpipes and voices shouting commands, the clatter of thousands of hooves was heard on the cobblestones.

Two devastating engagements started within hours of the last quadrille at the Duchess of Richmond's ball. At dawn on Friday 16 June the 42nd and 92nd Highlanders, led by their pipers, marched in the direction of Quatre-Bras. Twenty miles south of Brussels at Ligny, another battle against the Prussians began. Mounted since dawn to direct operations, Napoleon stayed in the saddle for a staggering eighteen hours before he returned to his headquarters at Charleroi.

The Prussian troops were led by the seventy-four-year-old Blücher, whose horse was shot from under him and whose army was forced to retreat. Although Marshal Grouchy was ordered to pursue Blücher's army, he soon lost sight of it.

Fifteen miles away at Quatre-Bras the French had a further triumph when Ney forced Wellington back towards the village of Waterloo. Both battles were in Napoleon's favour, but were not decisive. Apprehension in Brussels started an exodus of refugees on the road north to Antwerp. The road south from the battlefield was congested with returning ammunition carts laden with the wounded.

Buoyed up by two days of near victories, on the eve of the Battle of Waterloo, Napoleon asserted he had a 90 per cent chance of winning the next day. But it rained. A violent, almost tropical thunderstorm during the night drenched the soldiers on both sides – only a few had tents – and created deep mud. Clothes, men and muskets were soaked.

On Sunday 18 June Napoleon came face to face with the British – a personal confrontation which he had wanted since 1803 when he planned to invade across the English Channel with 2,000 boats. The battle would take place in an area of only 26,600 square metres (about three and a half square miles) on Mont St Jean, 16 kilometres south of Brussels. Among Wellington's generals was Napoleon's old foe from Corsica, Carlo Pozzo di Borgo. Also present, but not wanted by Wellington, was another of Napoleon's old antagonists, Sir William Sidney Smith.

Napoleon and Wellington were within a few months of being the same age, forty-six. Napoleon wore a grey *surtout* over the green uniform of the Chasseurs of the Guard and a violet waistcoat and pantaloons. Wellington eschewed uniform for a blue coat and white breeches, and, as always, was dressed immaculately. The Duke, contrary to popular belief, was only six inches taller than Napoleon, although he had the appearance of being much taller because of his slim figure and ram-rod straight deportment, while Napoleon was overweight and slightly stooped. Napoleon was five foot three inches tall, Wellington five foot nine inches. Napoleon, ruler and head of the French army, was accountable to nobody. Wellington, while in charge of his army, also took instructions from Lord Liverpool's government in London.

The two leaders had different attitudes to their soldiers. Napoleon, who had abolished flogging, always made an effort to get along with his men and had a genuine affinity with the common soldier. Wellington, hampered by his superior attitude to the lower classes, was more remote from his men. He stood apart as a man of wealth, rank and success. Because he was a brilliant tactician his men esteemed and followed him, whereas Napoleon's men followed him through affection. Wellington's men also respected him for his courage; he was known persistently to risk his own life alongside his soldiers. It was said that the sight of his long nose on the battlefield raised his men's spirits.

The personal mounts of Wellington and Napoleon, too, could hardly have been more different. Wellington rode Copenhagen, a bright chestnut stallion of 15.1 hands, named by General Grosvenor after the British victory in 1801. He was sired by Meteor, who came second in the Derby of 1786, and was a son of the renowned racehorse Eclipse. Grosvenor had been so impressed by Copenhagen's hollow back, powerful build, good looks and speed that he put him into training for the racetrack. After thirteen races Copenhagen was said to be a failure. He had won only one minor race at Newmarket and a sweepstake at Huntington. Sold to Sir Charles Stewart, he was shipped off to Spain with other horses for the Peninsular campaign. Wellington purchased him for £300 when he was five. Despite suffering hunger and appalling conditions, Copenhagen soon became Wellington's main horse and was seen with him both in battle and hunting with his pack of eight couple of hounds.

Which horse was Napoleon riding? Marengo? Had Ali been brought back from the stud? It seems that Jaffa had been retrieved from his stud and that Désirée, Cerbère and Marie were definitely there. So many of Napoleon's horses were dirty grey in colour and similar in appearance that it is easy to see how mistakes could have been made about their identification, especially from a distance. Napoleon's head saddler, Vincent, in a manuscript in the archives at Montpellier, wrote that Tauris, who had 'done the campaign of the North, had entered into Moscow, had gone to Elba and had come back to Paris, was at Waterloo and ridden by him'. Countless books published in England say that Napoleon rode Marengo. Marengo's courageous role is emphasised by J. M. Brereton in *The Horse in War*: 'The most celebrated horses of the Napoleonic wars are the personal chargers – Marengo and Copenhagen – of the two opposing commanders.' But the question remains: who was Marengo? So much has been written about the excellence of Napoleon's cavalry and the strength it gave to his army, yet information about which horse Napoleon was riding is often confusing. Brereton goes on:

Napoleon had acquired at least seven Arab horses during his Egyptian and Syrian campaigns ... But the one which, rightly or wrongly, has always outshone the others in public esteem is Marengo. A pure-bred Arabian he was a grey stallion ... if Meissionier and other artists have portrayed him as a much more imposing animal, it was considered almost *lèse-majesté* to show a great conqueror mounted on a pony.

Copenhagen was less than a third of the age of Napoleon's horses, which were all around twenty, around the average life expectancy of horses. Like other nineteenth-century English Thoroughbreds, Copenhagen retained the strong Arab characteristics of endurance, speed and loyalty with a certain independence. He often greeted Wellington's troops with excited neighs, but the men never stood too close to him as he was known sometimes to kick strangers. Was it possible that the horses facing each other were cousins? Could there be any truth in the rumour that Marengo, like Copenhagen, was a grandson of the mighty Eclipse?

15

The Last Battle: Waterloo

The barbarians, seeing the intention of the
Romans [about to land] sent out their horsemen
and charioteers, which they are accustomed to
use in warfare, followed by the rest of their force,
and attempted to prevent our disembarking.

JULIUS CAESAR,
Galic Wars, Book IV, 24 (The first known reference to
the horse in the British Isles)

Nearly 16,000 horsemen under Napoleon and some 12,500 under
Wellington faced each other on that fatal Sunday. Disregarding Spain
and Portugal, where the terrain was unsuitable for fighting on
horseback, Waterloo had the lowest turnout of French horsemen in
any major battle commanded by Napoleon in the previous eight
years. During the fifteen years of the Napoleonic Wars the cavalry
had peaked and was now on its downward curve. In 1800, at the
Battle of Marengo, Napoleon had had somewhere between 2,500 and
3,500 cavalry – the numbers differ. Five years later at the Battle of
Austerlitz the figure was about double this, and at the Battle of Jena

there were around 8,000. From then onwards the numbers of horse-men escalated, with a total of some 16,000 cavalry at Eylau in 1807, nearly 20,500 at Friedland in the same year but dropping to 13,000 at Wagram in 1809. The largest number of horses used in battle was at Borodino in 1812 with over 30,000 horsemen. After that the problem which had dogged Napoleon all his life – never having enough good horses – meant that the numbers in the cavalry could not be kept up. Despite the shortage of mounts, Napoleon had around 23,000 horsemen at the disastrous Battle of Leipzig in 1813, so at Waterloo he had around 7,000 fewer horses than at his previous battle.

Ready for the fray ahead, the eager men of the British cavalry were ordered to grind the backs of their swords so that they could use both edges when contending with the large number of French Cuirassiers in their steel armour. Soldiers and horses forced themselves through shoulder-high stalks of rye. The tall crops at first obscured the opposing sides from each other, but the men waited. And waited. Napoleon's first error was to postpone the start of the battle because of the wet ground and mud. Already wheels were sinking up to their axles. Knowing that horses, men and cannon would get stuck or slip, he deferred the attack in the hope that the ground would dry out. At Austerlitz he had delayed by six hours and won, but at Waterloo the four-hours gave the Prussians time to march from nearby Ligny. To the sound of rolling drums, trumpets and clarinets, with the bands playing 'Veillons au salut de l'empire', Napoleon reviewed his troops at ten a.m. The soldiers advanced slowly in eleven columns, each unit behind its fluttering flag, spreading themselves in long rows across the plain. They were ready for a frontal attack. With banners, gleaming eagles and the bright colours of the uniforms, from afar they were a magnificent sight – but the men were hungry and weary from their dreadful night in the rain and their horses were up to their fetlocks in mud. The food wagons were still miles behind, so the men had brandy but no bread.

One of the hundreds of lithographs printed in England after the Battle of Waterloo.

Wellington's troops were drawn up in his favourite position, behind a long ridge. The first shots were fired at 11.35. To clear his path, Napoleon attacked to break the right and left prongs, but the English repulsed both attacks. At about one p.m. Napoleon launched d'Erlon's corps of 16,000 men in a great charge of four long columns, following a massed artillery bombardment. So great was the noise of gunfire that the battle could be heard ten miles away in Brussels. The English infantry fought back furious charges by the French horsemen.

Napoleon was seen walking in obvious distress, and spent more of the day out of the saddle than in it. Instead of being on horseback throughout the battle as was his practice, he spent part of the time commanding operations sitting on a stool at a collapsible card table. At other times he sat either in his bullet-proof carriage or an open carriage. Nevertheless, R. H. Gronow in his *Reminiscences and Recollections*, (1990) wrote of the Battle of Waterloo: 'I recollect distinctly being able to see Bonaparte and his staff; and some of my brother officers using the glass, exclaim, "There he is on his white horse." '

When historians write about the 'enigma of Waterloo', among the reasons given for the defeat of Napoleon are his out-of-character indecision and his physical discomfort. Bladder problems are cited as a contributory reason for his poor performance. His cavalry escort often saw him waiting patiently to pass water and Prince Jerome Bonaparte said that Napoleon suffered at Waterloo from a disease of the bladder. These complaints were confirmed on St Helena when his autopsy noted urinary stones and other physical changes. Bladder irritations and haemorrhoids were problems. Dr Keynes added: 'His bladder changes were infinitely worse than stones. He had severe cystitis. Also riding on a horse was excruciatingly painful for him because of thrombosed internal piles.' But historian Dr Jean-François Lemaire, a leading expert on Napoleon's health and former Professor of Medicine at the Sorbonne, refutes the suggestion that Napoleon was physically and mentally diminished at the time of Waterloo:

> There is some evidence that after returning from Elba Napoleon suffered from some urinary disorder, probably a recurrence of the problems which plagued him much of his life. These and many other factors may have contributed to his fatigue on the day of the battle but, as regards his mental capacity, there is no medical evidence whatever that he was diminished at this period.

Later, Napoleon said that if he had not been so fatigued at Waterloo he would have ridden on horseback the whole night before the battle as was his habit. He had always spent the day and night before a battle reconnoitring the forces and position of the enemy, studying the field of battle, visiting the bivouacs and giving orders.

The French cannon thundered out against the English positions. Wellington's squares of well-drilled Anglo-German infantry repulsed cavalry charge after cavalry charge. The Scots Greys, screaming 'Forward! Forward!', came from behind and rode round and through the 92nd Highlanders.

The Duke of Richmond had ridden out with many sightseers to watch the battle and was present when the order was given for the famous charge of the Union and Household Brigades. This was spearheaded by the Scots and resulted in slaughter and chaos on both sides, yet the performance of the seven British cavalry brigades in the battle was a surprise. They were not well trained nor were their horses of good quality, but their fiery and ferocious spirit was evident.

So dense was the suffocating greyish-blue smoke that much of the battle in the afternoon was fought in semi-darkness. At 3.30 p.m. Ney, fighting like a madman in order to prove his loyalty to his Emperor, threw Kellermann's cavalry into a win-or-death advance. At the head of thousands of horses he dashed across the shallow dip between the two ridges. The terrifying Cuirassiers and their horses broke right through the 69th regiment, cutting down two entire English companies.

Later, Wellington said to his officers: 'Gentlemen, you might ignore what is currently the best cavalry in Europe. It is the most ill-mounted of all, the French cavalry. Since I have had personally to sustain the effect of its audacity (valour) and determination I know of no other which would be able to surpass it.'

Every move until about 4.30 p.m. gave Napoleon added confidence in the outcome. Blücher, mumbling excuses for smelling of gin and rhubarb juice, finally arrived with his army. Although exhausted from fighting eighteen hours the previous day and walking since dawn, his army pitched in. Later, Napoleon remarked mournfully: 'But for the arrival of General Blücher . . .'

Napoleon ordered Kellermann's Cuirassiers to make a final cavalry assault, which left the French with no reserves. Three thousand five hundred men on horseback – twenty-six squadrons – formed a line half a mile long and charged. In their way was an unknown sunken road. The first line of horses was on top of the obstacle before being aware of it. Too late they tried to stop, to avoid the high-banked rutted lane. As they fell, they could sense the second line toppling on top of them. Nobody described the horror better than Victor Hugo:

> the horses reared, threw themselves over, fell upon their backs, and struggled with their feet in the air, piling up and overturning their riders . . . The inexorable ravine could not yield until it was filled; riders and horses rolled in together pell-mell, grinding each other, making common flesh in this dreadful gulf, and when this grave was full of living men, the rest marched over them and passed on . . . Here the loss of the battle began.

The men in the British infantry squares were ordered to shoot at the horses, knowing that this would bring their riders down because the weight of their armour meant that once they were on their backs the men were like turtles and unable to get up. The French took no infantry support on their final massed cavalry charge against the British infantry squares, so both men and horses were decimated.

General Ney had his fifth horse of the day shot from under him. Companies, even regiments, were hidden from one another by gunsmoke. Refusing to admit defeat, Napoleon fought on. He held by his touchstone, the glorious Battle of Marengo, which had been lost in the late afternoon and had then turned around in his favour. After the arrival of Blücher, though, the British started to win the battle. Both the Prussians and the tactical expertise of Wellington were crucial to victory.

Wellington rode up to the crest, raising his hat to signal his men to advance in a general counterstroke. The British poured down the slope, sweeping Napoleon's shattered army before them. The Prussians surged in from the side. As the sun set, the darkness started to swallow not only an army but an empire. The Napoleonic Wars and the last momentous battle between France and Britain were over. Night was falling when the command '*La Garde recule!*' reverberated through the noise and haze. The battle was summed up by Wellington: 'The nearest run thing you ever saw in your life.' As Hugo wrote: 'the sky had been overcast all day, but at eight o'clock it cleared to allow the sinister red light of the setting sun to flood through the elms on the Nivelles road – the same sun that had risen at Austerlitz.'

A few of the faithful old guard continued fighting, long enough for Napoleon to get away. Somewhere in the darkness he and his horse were separated. His foolproof means of escape – a satchel of poison far more potent than the dose which had failed him before Elba – was still attached to his braces. In the indescribable confusion following the battle he rode alone, unrecognised in the stream of fugitives. The two imperial carriages containing his clothes, his money, his papers and Pauline's diamond necklace, were captured.

If Murat had led the charge at Waterloo the battle might have been won, but he had deserted his brother-in-law, changing sides before and after Elba; and if Berthier had been there, perhaps Napoleon would not have had to abandon the field.

The battlefield was covered with the dead. The groaning and screaming of the wounded was loud and never-ending. Men and horses waited either to be rescued by wagons or for the mercy of a pistol or bayonet, many preferring the second option. Crippled horses lay on the ground, bleeding and struggling, their legs kicking in pain. Some were sitting on their tails, dazed and whimpering. A few soldiers and farriers with axes put animals out of their agony. Later, one witness wrote:

> the whole field from right to left was a mass of dead bodies. In one spot, to the right of La Haye Sainte, the French Cuirassiers were literally piled on each other; many soldiers not wounded lying under their horses; others, fearfully wounded, occasionally with their horses struggling upon their wounded bodies. The sight was sickening, and I had no means or power to assist them.

Wellington had not changed horses throughout the whole day, yet at the end of the battle Copenhagen did not seem exhausted when led back to the stables at the British headquarters in the village of Waterloo. He had carried his master for fifteen hours, as he had the previous day. His only gesture of relief came when Wellington dismounted. He kicked out, almost incapacitating the man he had taken to triumph. Wellington later praised him: 'There may be faster horses, no doubt many handsomer, but for bottom and endurance I never saw this fellow.' At Waterloo Wellington wrote the victory dispatches to be rushed to London.

After the battle General Blücher took possession of Marie, named after the Countess Walewska; Cerbère was found dead, hit by a cannon ball; no one is sure what happened to the little grey mare Désirée, named after Napoleon's first fiancée. The RUSI catalogue states that Marengo was 'at Waterloo in 1815, when he was wounded in the near hip. After Napoleon's defeat at Waterloo, Lord Petre gained possession of the horse.'

But no Lord Petre is listed among the serving officers at Waterloo. He was not on the guest list for the Duchess of Richmond's ball, nor was he one of the civilians, like the Duke of Richmond, who went to the battlefield. For Lord Petre was not there. However, a cousin of his fought at Waterloo, twenty-four-year-old Henry Petre, a Lieutenant in the 6th (Inniskilling) Dragoons, a nephew of the late Lord Petre and member of the Dunkenhalgh branch of the family from Lancashire. He is said to have recognised the horse's imperial 'N' and laurel-leafed crown emblazoned on his rump and the bee motif stamped on his harness, saved him from the looters, tended to his wound and led him to the village of Waterloo. But was the horse really Marengo? Whoever he was, now out of French hands he took on an English identity.

Peasants, looters and scavengers started to strip the corpses of everything of value, from weapons, blood-stained uniforms and boots to harnesses, horseshoes, saddles, even teeth to sell to dentists – for a long time dentures were known as 'Waterloo teeth'.

One soldier wrote:

By the light of the moon I picked my way among the bodies of my sleeping, as well as my dead comrades; but the horrors of the scene created such a terror in my mind . . . a horse was lying dead on its side, and a man sitting upright with his back against the horse's body, I thought I heard the man call to me . . . placing my left hand on his shoulder, [I] attempted to lift him up with my right; my hand, however, passed through his body, and I then saw that both he and his horse had been killed by a cannonball.

The following morning over 50,000 animal and human corpses were almost stripped bare. In this terrible sea of nakedness nothing differentiated the victors from the vanquished, whether horse or human, apart from the shorter, docked tails of the British horses. Thousands of wounded lay gasping for water or death.

One stripped man slowly recovered consciousness and awoke, but was unable to crawl more than a few inches, his pain excruciating. Day after day gangrene spread from where a bullet was lodged in his right arm. He was Napoleon's twenty-six-year-old Dutch coachman.

Five days later an English officer, finding him nearly dead from thirst and blood loss, took him to Brussels to have his right arm amputated. He lived to tell the tale.

Brussels emptied. Most of the British troops and the surviving 9,000 horses started the march south. Copenhagen went towards Paris with Wellington. Both Napoleon and two of his old horses were soon to be heading towards England on different ships. The horse captured and known to history as Marengo sailed for a new country, fresh fields and fame. Napoleon was in Paris, but was soon to be a prisoner of war, sailing close to the shores of England, but never landing.

It is probable that Jaffa and Marengo were put aboard a ship with the wounded horses of the Household Brigade of cavalry, which were repatriated to England while their healthy comrades made their triumphal march on Paris.

16

Marengo Goes to England

Still sate the warrior, saddle fast,
Till, stumbling in the mortal shock,
Down went the steed, the girthing broke,
Hurled in a heap lay man and horse.

G. J. WHYTE MELVILLE,
'Riding Recollections'

After Napoleon abdicated he retreated to Malmaison. Between 25 and 29 June dozens of gendarmes patrolled the estate's boundaries. Blücher's flying column of Prussians, determined to seize Napoleon dead or alive, were on their way, out for revenge and loot. Wellington's troops arrived in Paris with Louis XVIII – and the vital constitutional charter – in their baggage train. A campaign had been started against those who changed sides during Napoleon's hundred days, and a ban was being put in place on any publicity that would raise support for Napoleon.

Napoleon left Malmaison for Rochefort on the Atlantic coast early on the 29th, the same day that the remnants of his defeated army staggered into Paris. With a heavy heart he began the journey to his second exile. With him were generals, officers, chamberlains, the Countess de Montholon and the Countess Bertrand, twenty Berlin travelling carriages crowded with servants and overloaded with luggage including books, silverware, pictures, papers, Sèvres china, clothes, his metal campaign bed, even his son's little bronze cannon. The dust created by the vehicles and the horses filled the air. By then Marengo was either on his way to England or had already arrived.

At Rochefort Napoleon's options narrowed to three: escape to America on a brig waiting to brave the blockade; an exchange of identity with his brother Joseph who had offered to swap places; or surrender to his old enemy, the English. Looming in the distance, like a ghost from the past, was the seventy-four-gun *Bellerophon*, the ship that had been a symbol of defeat for him at the Battles of the Nile and Trafalgar.

On 15 July Napoleon dressed himself in the green uniform of the Chasseurs of the Imperial Guard and threw himself on the mercy of Captain Maitland of the *Bellerophon*. Napoleon had written to the Prince Regent asking for asylum in England, saying that he was 'Themistocles, come to claim a seat by the hearth of the British people'.

Nine days later, when the *Bellerophon* arrived off the English coast, Napoleon was kept at sea. The ship anchored at the picturesque port of Torbay, but the Emperor was forbidden to set foot on English soil. A large flotilla of curious onlookers soon invaded the harbour. In hired rowing boats, skiffs, dinghies, launches and fishing smacks, thousands went as close to the ship as they dared, to catch a glimpse of the short, stout figure in his long grey coat and cocked hat, pacing the deck with his hands behind his back. Whenever Napoleon observed a well-dressed woman in the crowded boats he pulled off his hat and bowed. So immense were the crowds around the ship that the sailors adopted theatrical-type cue-boards to inform them of the principal actor's next appearance. Placards announced he was 'in his cabin', or 'about to go up on deck'.

The ship then sailed for Plymouth, where it was met by another noisy multitude. Sadly, two girls drowned in the disorderly rush of boats, which brought 10,000 curious sightseers a day to see Napoleon. The *Morning Post* on 8 August wrote that 'a large portion of the spectators not only took off their hats, but cheered him, apparently with the view of soothing his fallen fortunes and treating him with respect and consideration'. Alarmed by his popularity, the government hastened its plans for his departure to St Helena and he was trans-shipped to the *Northumberland*.

Napoleon guessed that if he could only manage to get ashore he had a fair chance of gaining widespread popularity. Even Admiral Lord Keith muttered: 'D—n the fellow! If he had obtained an interview with H.R.H. [Prince Regent] in half an hour they would have been the best friends in Europe.' But while many Whigs and Radicals had sympathy for him, the conservatives, the Tories, who were in power, were terrified by this wave of support. They feared not only Napoleon himself but the doctrine of the Revolution. Lord Liverpool wrote to Castlereagh: 'You know enough of the feelings of people in this country not to doubt he would become an object of curiosity immediately, and possibly of compassion, in the course of a few months.'

Napoleon was adamant that he was not a prisoner of war but a ruler who had surrendered and said when he heard of his destination:

I would not live three months. With my habits and my constitution it would be immediate death. I am in the habit of riding twenty leagues on horseback every day. On this minuscule rock at the end of the world what will I do? The weather will be too strong for me. No I shall not go to St Helena. Botany Bay would be preferable to St Helena.

Blücher, of course, had another more radical solution – the firing squad. However, this would not have gained the approval of the Duke of Wellington, whose admiration for Napoleon can still be seen in his London house to this day.

On 8 August the *Northumberland* weighed anchor. The question needs to be asked here why Marengo did not belong to the British government after being taken at Waterloo. Why was he not sent to St Helena with Napoleon? The British government allowed Napoleon to take two of his personal horses from the imperial stables in France to his exile in the Atlantic Ocean.

As Napoleon sailed away, a huge show in London was getting under way displaying one of his favourite possessions. A Prussian major, having captured Napoleon's coach complete with its four large brown horses, handed it over to Blücher, who presented it to the Prince of Wales. The government came to an arrangement with William Bullock to display it at his museum, in the Egyptian Hall, Piccadilly. With its bullet-proof panels and silver-gilt furniture sprinkled with bees and the laurel-crowned letter 'N', the carriage caused a sensation. More than 10,000 people a month paid a shilling each to see and touch this elaborate vehicle, which was large enough for Napoleon to sleep, work and eat in. Among the spectators who willingly paid extra to climb inside, two by two, so they could boast that they had sat where Napoleon had sat on the silk couch which folded up and down, were Captain Howard's wife and two of their daughters. So immense was the gawking mob climbing over it that it became a favourite subject for the cartoonists Rowlandson and Cruikshank. Lord Byron himself showed his admiration of Napoleon by ordering a well-known coachbuilder in Long Acre, Charles Baxter, to build him a replica of the coach for his personal use.

Although it is often said that Marengo was displayed at Bullock's museum, this was not the case; his exact whereabouts at this stage are not known. The only imperial horses on show there were the four carriage horses accompanied by Napoleon's former coachman who had lain with the dead and lost his arm at Waterloo. A booklet on sale described the coach, adding that it had carried the Emperor to Russia, to Elba, and 'bore him to the fatal field of Waterloo!'

> Four of the horses which drew the Ex-Emperor, still remain with the carriage; they are supposed to be of Norman breed: they are of a brown colour; of good size; and each appears to combine more strength, speed, and spirit, than are generally found together in one animal. Till their arrival in England they were in all seasons exposed to the weather; to this is attributed their preservation during the horrors of the retreat in which they assuredly bore a part.

The leaflet added that the horses were also on the horrendous campaign to Russia:

> The harness is very little worthy of an Imperial equipage; it bears strong marks of its service in the Russian campaign, and its former uses are to be recognized only by the bees, arms, and eagles, which are to be seen in several places.

The most controversial objects among the silver-gilt furniture and the scarlet valises were the most trivial – not the silver chamber pot, not Napoleon's sister's diamond necklace, but, according to the booklet, 'some Windsor-soap, and some English court-plaister'. The soap was indisputably English. Despite the massive trade embargo he had imposed against Britain, despite his invasion of Russia when the Tsar broke the blockade, despite his efforts to help the soap workers at Marseilles, Napoleon had succumbed a little to what he had fought to suppress during his reign, the fashion for things English. In his trade war against Britain he banned his wife Josephine from wearing English

BONAPARTE'S
White Barb CHARGER,
MARENGO,
Has been inspected by many of the Nobility and Gentry,
And is NOW EXHIBITING at the WATERLOO ROOMS,
No. 94, PALL MALL.

This beautiful white Barb Charger was the favourite Horse of the late Emperor, and accompanied him through most of his Battles. He has five Wounds which are visible; and a Bullet still remains in his Tail. The Imperial Crown and the Letter N are branded on his hind Quarters. He is so gentle, that the most timid Lady may approach him without fear.

The superb Saddle and Bridle and the Boots that Napoleon wore at Moscow, are likewise shown.

The Person who exhibits the Horse, is well acquainted with the Movements of the late Emperor, and speaks six different Languages.

J. and C. Adlard Printers, 23, Bartholomew Close.

Admittance, Ladies and Gentlemen, 1s. Children and Servants, 6d.

Handbill advertising Marengo as exhibit at the Waterloo Rooms.

muslin, developed the crop of sugar beet as an alternative to sugar cane from the West Indies, promoted the use of chicory instead of coffee and tisanes instead of tea, introduced a mixture of clay and graphite to replace the lead in pencils and turned local timbers such as oak, elm and ash into fashionable alternatives to mahogany, which came from British colonies. To reduce the desire for mahogany, he had promoted the use of ornate furniture, painted white or grey with features picked out in gold or completely gilded. But now he had been caught out with a bar of finest English soap. So damning was the soap that some of Napoleon's supporters claimed that it could not have belonged to him, but had been planted there by Bourbon sympathisers.

Meanwhile, the maimed and wounded soldiers from makeshift hospitals in Brussels were being repatriated to Britain and the wounded horses of the Household Brigade were sold by auction. The amount of training that went into cavalry horses, as well as their suffering, was shown by this poignant story of Sir Astley Cooper, the surgeon who sat on the board of examiners at the Veterinary College in London. Distressed by the hardship these heroic horses had endured, he purchased the twelve most badly wounded. Slowly and painfully, with assistance from his students, he extracted bullets and grapeshot from their bodies and limbs. After their recovery he let them loose in his park and was delighted one morning to see them form in line, charge and then retreat, and afterwards gallop about. They repeated these manoeuvres every morning.

Waterloo had already become a place of pilgrimage. Among the sightseers was Sir Walter Scott, soon to write his masterpiece, *The Life of Napoleon.* Relics of the battlefield were pressed upon him by peasants. All that was left on the ground were the bones of horses, hats, rags and scraps of leather and uniforms, account books, prayerbooks and papers. Some tourists even collected peach stones and filberts so they could plant Waterloo trees in their gardens at home in England. When Victor Hugo later came to the battlefield to immortalise the place in *Les Misérables*, he wrote: 'Almost on the spot where [Napoleon's] horse stood, cannon-balls, old sabre blades, and shapeless rust-eaten projectiles have been picked up.' He aptly summed up the battle: 'Waterloo was not a victory, but a change in the direction of the world.'

17

Napoleomania

Not a word to each other; we kept the great pace
Neck by neck, stride by stride, never changing
*   our place;*
I turned in my saddle and made its girths tight,
Then shortened each stirrup, and set the pique
*   right,*
Rebuckled the cheek-strap, chained slacker the
*   bit,*
Nor galloped less steadily Roland a whit.

ROBERT BROWNING,
'How They Brought the Good News from Ghent to
Aix'

Ney was condemned for high treason and executed in Paris and Murat was shot by a firing squad in Naples, while Napoleon, sick and lonely, deteriorated slowly beneath the tropical sun on St Helena. Marengo fared better in his captivity in England because of the British public's continued and ambivalent fascination with his ex-master. A visitor to London might have had trouble working out who was the greater hero in British eyes, Wellington or Napoleon. It was hard to believe that England had so recently been Napoleon's indomitable and bitter enemy. Some people venerated him, many still loathed his memory, while others were merely intrigued by him; no one was indifferent. He became the Englishman's favourite foreigner, a fallen idol who could now be safely admired from afar. Many, of course, continued to see him as 'Boney' the ogre, warmonger, usurper and tyrant.

The Napoleonic legend was fuelled by exhibitions, publications, paintings and prints. The crowds kept on paying to view Napoleonic memorabilia – despite an economic slump caused by a catastrophically poor harvest in 1816 and the ending of the trade blockade, which brought on to the British market quantities of competitively priced goods. The success of such shows was due to an often barely literate population wanting to see more, hear more, ultimately wanting a physical link to great events. News sheets carried stories, but few outside London or Paris were illustrated.

While Napoleon's grand coach at Bullock's Museum pulled in the crowds, at the other end of Piccadilly his towering nude statue – complete with Republican fig leaf – dominated the entrance of the London home of the Duke of Wellington, Apsley House. Then, as now, the visitor to the stone mansion at Hyde Park Corner was greeted by the eleven-and-a-half-feet high *chef d'oeuvre* by Canova. It had so embarrassed Napoleon when he saw it that he had it hidden in a cupboard at the Louvre. During Louis XVIII's reign the statue was sold to the British government and was presented to the Iron Duke, who had already accumulated a selection of Bonaparte memorabilia, including portraits, china and silverware. He even slept in a bed that had once belonged to Napoleon. W. A. Fraser, who visited Apsley House, wrote that the Duke 'slept as far away from the Duchess as he could' and his bedroom:

A Thomas Rowlandson cartoon of the exhibition at Bullock's Museum showing Napoleon's carriage taken at Waterloo.

could hardly be dignified by the name of room: it was a closet. The bed was one that had belonged to Napoleon, and was in the style of the Empire. Any one in the least taller than the Duke could not have lain at full length upon it; it looked very uncomfortable; the head of the bed was close to the half-door.

After Waterloo writers, biographers, even philosophers, continued to sing Napoleon's praises. Hegel's celebration of him as 'world soul' was taken up by Nietzsche, while Goethe never revised his belief in Napoleon as an indomitable character, the equivalent of a Greek demi-god. In Britain books about Napoleon were published and sold swiftly, whereas in France fines and prison terms were imposed on journalists and writers who incited people to follow him. The songwriter Auguste Barthélemy was jailed for alluding to the former Emperor in the lines of a popular lyric. Even pictures of the flower which had become closely associated with Napoleon, the violet, were considered subversive. Mademoiselle Georges, despite her fling with Wellington, continued to show her loyalty to Napoleon and defiantly wore violets as a corsage. Her defiance forced her to resign from the Comédie-Française. The anti-Napoleon ban, initiated by the restored Louis XVIII, continued until the final departure of the Bourbons in 1830.

Contrary to his pessimistic prediction that he would survive in exile for only a few months, Napoleon lived on for six unhappy years. The long journey across the Atlantic prevented the news of his death on 5 May 1821 on St Helena from reaching London quickly. Nearly two months passed before the notice of his demise appeared in *The Times* and other London newspapers. One article, headed 'Bonaparte is No More', said that after forty days of lingering illness, the General had expired painlessly, in his fifty-second year, of the same disease which had carried off his father – stomach cancer. The news of Napoleon's death brought different reactions: relief, jubilation, even sorrow, but definitely renewed interest in him. Already Wellington was regretting the political outcome of his victory. In 1821 he expressed his admiration of Napoleon to Princess Lieven: 'We made a tremendous mistake in getting rid of Napoleon. He is the man we ought to have had. As long as the Bourbons hold four thrones there will be no peace in Europe. None of that family is any good.' Wellington might not have been so generous had he been aware of Napoleon's degenerating condition. Because of his endocrine problem, whether in war or at peace, it is unlikely that he could have continued to rule wisely.

The artist Benjamin Robert Haydon, exploiting the insatiable passion for anything Napoleonic, sold forty portraits of the Emperor in England, including one to the English statesman Sir Robert Peel.

The myth lived on: Napoleon on a white horse, drawn by Henri Toulouse-Lautrec, seventy years after the Emperor's death.

On New Year's Day 1824 Haydon spent a day doing the shows, first the Panorama of Pompeii then the Waterloo Rooms in Pall Mall to see Marengo. A year earlier Marengo had suddenly appeared in London as the star attraction at the Waterloo Rooms. As the records point to him first being on show then, the possibility exists that Marengo had gone to St Helena. But there is no evidence to support such a theory. It appears that only two French horses accompanied Napoleon to St Helena and according to records in France they were Tauris and Coquet. However, this does not agree with the records of the Musée de l'Armée, which say that Vizir went to St Helena. Indeed, the identities of the horses that went with Napoleon vary in different publications. It appears that during Napoleon's imprisonment Tauris was leading a happy and contented life in France. A horse by the name of Cheik seems to have been the horse with an empty saddle which followed the funeral procession on St Helena, but there is no record of a horse by that name going to Rochefort, let alone St Helena. There is, of course, the possibility that Cheik was one of the four riding horses sent from the Cape of Good Hope to Napoleon on St Helena and may have been given the name of an old favourite.

Longing to boast that he had straddled the special horse of the former conqueror, Haydon wrote in his diary that he was determined to 'have a mount & shall when the room is less crowded'. But Marengo resisted this final dishonour. Who owned the Waterloo Rooms at that time and who owned Marengo is difficult to work out: 94 Pall Mall is not listed in the Poor Rates records at the City of Westminster archives. To confuse matters, 94 Pall Mall belonged to a succession of owners between 1815 and 1825 and the buildings along this stretch on the south side of the road were subject to renumbering. In 1815, 94 was most likely unoccupied as it is not listed, but five years later it appears under the ownership of William Dennison and the Marquis of Buckingham. The Angersteins, the family who were soon to play a prominent part in the life and myth of Marengo, are listed in 1815 as living in 103, in 1820 at 102 and in 1823 as living at 100. In 1824 the list remains as above, but there are three notable amendments which were crossed out on the original documents, so we can presume that the buildings changed occupancy during the course of the year. At 94 the name is crossed out and replaced by George Adams, and 100 is amended to the new National Gallery. George Adams was a member of J. & G. Adams, a family firm of carriage-makers whose main premises were at 28 Haymarket. It seems likely that they converted a large showroom suitable for carriages into a 'lounge' in which to exhibit Marengo. And it seems likely that the man exhibiting Marengo was Captain Henry Howard. The archives at the Guildhall Library contain a few more clues, including a handbill dated 1822 advertising an exhibition under the patronage of HRH The Princess Augusta at the Waterloo Rooms, 94 Pall Mall. By 1826 the name of these premises had been changed to the Grand Salon.

The next date with which Marengo can be linked is 21 April 1824. A letter in the Royal Archives from James Ward to Sir William Knighton asks for the name of the horse which George IV wanted him to paint:

> I am about to procure the Portrait of Bonaparte's Charger before he leaves London again – the Horse is in Dorset Mews, Dorset Square – after that I shall be anxious to get that of His Majesty's. I wish to know the Name of that Horse and also if I should paint it at Windsor or in the stables of Carlton Palace.
>
> His Majesty in His great kindness and condescension mentioned the accompaniments of the saddle &c &c. I should desire much after procuring the portrait to make a subject . . .

There is, alas, no surviving reply to this letter, and no lead to help sort out its ambiguity. Does Ward's sentence: 'I wish to know the Name of that Horse and also if I should paint it at Windsor or in the stables of Carlton Palace,' refer to Napoleon's horse or George IV's horse? Had Marengo merged his imperial connections in France with royal links in England? It is stated in *The Horse in Art and History*, edited by Michael Seth-Smith (1978), that

> when the Regent succeeded to the throne he commissioned Ward to paint three of his horses, Monitor, Soothsayer, and Nonpareil. Their portraits still hang in the Royal collection at Buckingham Palace. Ward recorded that he disputed with the King about the correct action of a horse in one of his pictures, but he was nevertheless granted permission to study Napoleon's charger Marengo at Windsor Castle. The Emperor's white Barb lives for ever in the painting James did of him.

It seems unlikely that Marengo was kept at Windsor, but in his amazing career nothing can be ruled out. If Marengo was not there, it has to be asked why Ward was writing to the royal family for their permission to paint Napoleon's horse. It was possible that he was trying to keep his reputation alive. Ward started his autobiography three times, but he never wrote more than a thousand words. Even so, he managed to contradict himself. His giant allegorical canvas of Waterloo for the walls of the Royal Hospital in Chelsea, painted after winning a competition run by the British Institution, nearly bankrupted him and was so badly received that he fell from popularity soon afterwards. When displayed at Bullock's exhibition room in the Egyptian Hall, it met with such derision that it ended up being cut up into separate paintings and, for the most part, lost.

Under each of his horse portraits Ward wrote a caption with a brief description of the horse, followed by the owner's name. But in the case of Captain Howard, written under Marengo's portrait, he omits to include a Christian name. With such a common surname and not even an initial, this could have been another mystery. Howard is the family name of the Dukes of Norfolk, the Earls of Effingham, the Earls of Carlisle, and, of course, many others. But, because of Marengo's connection with the Petre family, a search through *Debretts* shows that only one Howard was a contender. Henry Howard, Captain in the 1st York militia of Corby Castle, Cumberland, was closely related to the Petre family – the two families had intermarried for generations and continued to do so. Captain Henry Howard and his second wife, Catherine, had a son and three daughters. The second daughter, Emma Agnes, married the 11th Baron Petre as his second wife, while their third daughter, Adelina Maria, married her cousin, Henry Petre of Dunkenhalgh as his second wife. The connections were endless and it becomes clear how a horse could pass from one to another and how the name of Lord Petre became linked with Marengo. The Petres were a family of horse-lovers. Lord Petre had his own racetrack at Stapledon in Essex. An uncle, who was younger than him, Edward Petre of Stapledon Park, Yorkshire, had eleven horses in training, a couple of which were later sold to George IV.

Some published notes by a General Higginson, a racing man, written in the middle of the nineteenth century, insist that Marengo was actually Tauris. This, though, is impossible; Tauris came into Napoleon's stables only a year before the Battle of Wagram and does not fit in with what is known of Marengo, nor did he come from Egypt.

A favourite of Napoleon's Tauris had been given to one of his equerries, the Baron de Montaranby, by the Emperor before his departure for St Helena. The Baron purchased other distinguished horses and formed an equine guard of honour around Tauris. Tauris, aware of his preferential status, never lost pride of place in the Baron's affections. The former equerry was always proud to be seen riding him in Paris, even boasting that he was 'solicited by rich Englishmen who wanted to buy him'. Tauris died of old age in the Baron's stables at the Chateau de Beaurepaire. Later the Baron's widow gave away Tauris's skin which had been used as a carpet under her late husband's desk. Tauris was cherished – even to having his portrait painted with Roustam with the family chateau in the background.

Not unlike the way in which he had been passed from one cousin to another – from Petre to Howard – in 1824, Marengo now went from one neighbour to another. An unconnected event changed the course of his existence. The government paid £57,000 for thirty-four works of art from the estate of J. J. Angerstein, a financier in the City of London who had become an art collector of distinction. The paintings formed the nucleus of the new National Gallery's collection, which was housed in Angerstein's old house a few doors along from the Waterloo Rooms. While these paintings were being admired at the gallery's opening, Angerstein's son and grandson, both called John, put horses, including Marengo, to stud at New Barnes on the Isle of Ely in Cambridgeshire. He had three registered offspring, two colts and a filly called Araby who was out of an Anglo-Arab. None, alas, was any good on a racetrack. In *The Times* on 14 April 1932 a letter from Major Sandford states: 'A curious feature about Marengo was that he possessed that peculiar pigment in his blood which transferred to all his stock his own colour (grey), irrespective of their dams' coats.'

Marengo proved unsuitable for breeding and was eventually sent to the Angerstein country seat at Weeting Park with its lovely meadows and woods, near the leafy Suffolk village of Brandon. Marengo lived in eighteenth-century stables and was assured of every comfort.

In 1831, ten years after the death of Napoleon, his son, no longer referred to as the King of Rome but now the Duke of Reichstadt, died in his *cage dorée* in the palace of Schönbrunn in Vienna at the age of twenty-one. Marengo died the next year and his skeleton was sent to the London Hospital to be articulated so it could be put on public exhibition. This was not unusual for the time. In the same year, the body of Jeremy Bentham, the philosopher and social reformer, was also articulated so it could be displayed. (It is still on view at University College London.)

Why was Marengo fêted and immortalised while Jaffa, the other imperial horse who had come to England, ended his days in relative anonymity in the green fields of Kent? Purchased by a Mr Green at a Belgian auction after Waterloo, he had been taken to an ancient moated mansion two miles west of Cranbrook in Kent, in the little parish of Glassenbury, which Green was renting from Baron Nettleblat. To the great grief of his owner, Jaffa had to be put down in 1829. Jaffa was buried in the grounds with a small trunk of coins, but without his tail, which has since been lost. A memorial column was erected after his death: 'Under this stone lies Jaffa the charger of Napoleon aged 37 years.' But in 1965 when the then owner, Miss Roberts, asked the Territorial Army to dig up the grave, no bones were found, just two hooves with two horseshoes. The tin of coins, too, had disappeared. However, a metal detector indicated heavy traces of metal. Rumours immediately started that the skeleton had been taken to London. Miss Roberts erected a new headstone over the area where the horseshoes were found. Another complication to Jaffa's story is that, according to the archives in Paris, he was number 1992 in the imperial stables and came from Turkey, but countless modern references say he came from Egypt in 1799 and was again 'Napoleon's favourite horse'.

Copenhagen had the joy of staying with his master until the end. He was retired on the Duke's estate at Stratfield Saye in Hampshire, where he often wandered around the garden, the Duchess feeding him with his favourite bread. Four years after Marengo's death, Copenhagen died at the age of twenty-eight. Wellington flatly refused to allow him either to be stuffed or articulated and arranged a burial with full military honours on his estate. The night before he was to be lowered into his grave, a hoof was sawn from the corpse. When the

Duke discovered that his horse had lost his foot he burst into a terrible rage. After the Duke's death a contrite butler presented it to the second Duke, still wrapped in *The Times*, explaining that he had been too scared of the wrath of the first Duke to confess that he had stolen the horse's foot. The headstone of Copenhagen reads:

> Here lies Copenhagen, the charger ridden by the Duke of Wellington the entire day at the Battle of Waterloo. Born 1808 died 1836. God's humbler instrument, though meaner clay should share the glory of that glorious day.

The fact that Marengo was in London when the post-Waterloo Napoleonic industry began, ensured that he was at the forefront of the frenzied interest in all things Napoleonic. Two years before Marengo's death the growing fascination of the French for their ex-Emperor was permitted under Louis-Philippe. The new citizen-king, out to exploit the popularity of Napoleon, had his coffin repatriated from under the willows of St Helena to lie under the magnificent dome of the Hôtel des Invalides in Paris.

The return of Napoleon's remains to Paris in 1840 added fresh drama and sentiment to the legend of the white horse. The Emperor's coffin, encased in a colossal marble catafalque, surrounded with trophies, standards, fringed draperies and mourning statues and covered with the cloak he wore at the Battle of Marengo, was pulled by four rows of horses. In front walked a solitary white horse carrying nothing but Napoleon's empty saddle. His black boots were turned in the stirrups, in the traditional manner of the funeral parade. Emotions ran high. A shiver went through the crowds. 'It is Napoleon's battle horse,' they whispered. The myth lived.

Napoleon's apotheosis received a boost from unexpected directions, such as the very special state visit to Paris in August 1855 by George III's granddaughter, Queen Victoria – the first visit of a

British sovereign to Paris since 1431. Since 1842 she had been the patron of the RUSI Museum, where the skeleton of Marengo was on exhibition. In Paris one of the first things she did was ask to see the tomb of Napoleon. As she slowly descended from her carriage, old soldiers from the Napoleonic wars stood to attention, holding flaming torches. There was a sombre drum roll. The Queen quietly put her hand on her oldest son's shoulder, the fourteen-year-old Prince of Wales who was in full Highland dress, and said: 'Kneel down before the tomb of the great Napoleon.' Victoria wrote in her diary: 'There I stood before the coffin of England's bitterest foe; I, the granddaughter of that king who hated him most, and who vigorously opposed him . . . this solemn scene took place by torchlight, and during a thunderstorm.'

Just over thirty years later a stuffed horse, called Vizir (sometimes with the alternate spelling of 'Vizier') ended up in Paris and was later exhibited at Les Invalides when part of it became the Musée de l'Armée. There was some confusion about his exact identity, though, let alone his name. Few people were aware of the existence of this white horse with brown flecks until, on 29 June 1868, the Natural History Society of Manchester presented it to Napoleon's nephew, Napoleon III. Not knowing what to do with such a bulky exhibit, the new Emperor had it put in storage in the Louvre. How the naturalists of Manchester had acquired the horse and kept it for years and why they suddenly decided to send it back to France is another mystery. All we know is that during his first exile in England, before he seized power on 29 January 1839, Prince Louis Napoleon visited Manchester and inspected various factories and public buldings. Perhaps Marengo's celebrity status meant that there was no room for a rival attraction. The minutes of the Manchester Natural History Society noted on 25 January 1843 that 'the celebrated Arabian charger Vizier formerly property of Napoleon Buonaparte, presented by John Greaves, esq., of Staffordshire, is an interesting relic of that extraordinary man, and has attracted the attention of many visitors'. An article in *L'Eclair, Journal de Paris*, dated 4 February 1909, called 'Les Chevaux de Napoléon I' by Georges Montorgueil, says that Mr Greaves had obtained the stuffed horse from a Mr Clarke, who had obtained it from a Monsieur de Chaulaire near Boulogne, who got him no one knows where. It was said that a Sultan had given him to Napoleon and that his name was Vizir or Vizier and he had died in 1829. On 13 March 1868, the Natural History Society of Manchester noted 'the Report of the formal offer the horse Vizier to the Emperor of the French, after consultation with the Foreign Office'.

The romantic cult of Napoleon was here to stay. Indeed, so fashionable was the general infatuation that many boasted dubious, even imaginary, associations with him and his horse. Irish horse-breeders claimed Marengo as their own. This horse, they said, had come from Ireland. Even fifty years after Marengo's death an article in the journal of the Waterford and South-east of Ireland Archaeological Society reveals:

> Marengo . . . came from County Wexford and there is a stone in
> the field where he was born commemorating the event. Napoleon
> . . . sent his orders to procure one [an Irish horse] stipulating
> that it must not be a large horse, he being a short man. In order
> to evade the English blockade, the chosen horse was swum five
> miles out to sea, at dead of night, to a waiting French frigate.

But the article also says that Napoleon had sixty horses killed under him – when the figure was only around ten, eighteen at the most.

Marengo was sometimes said to be a cousin of Wellington's horse, Copenhagen; or that he was by Hidalgo, the grandson of the most famous of all racehorses, Eclipse; some said that he was a Thorough-bred not an Arab. Marengo's frail skeletal remains, however, give little credence to these wild theories.

While I was researching the history of Napoleon and his horses, it soon became clear that many aspects of Marengo's life have been embellished. Nowhere in any of the registers of the imperial stables, or for that matter in any primary sources in the archives in Paris, could I find a horse called Marengo – and there were a lot of horses and names; the register kept by Caulaincourt stops at horse number 1732 in June 1815. Following Napoleon's horses through their careers is puzzling. As explained earlier, their exact names are sometimes difficult to trace as, apart from nicknames, some horses were given new names and others were occasionally retitled with the names of deceased favourites. For example, the first Roitelet, number 323 in the register, arrived in the stables in 1805, and died ten years later. In May 1812 another horse arrived from the Italian stables and it too was called Roitelet, but is number 1238. Dr Jean-François Lemaire, a member of the board of the Institut Napoléon who was awarded the Grand Prix of the Fondation Napoléon in 1999, confirmed my doubts with the words: 'The French archives are silent about Marengo.' He added: 'It seems doubtful whether a horse could have survived from the Italian campaign until 1815.'

But the question needs to be asked: who was Marengo? Was he Ali under a different name? Did Napoleon give Ali the nickname 'Marengo'? He must have been a very special horse indeed if Napoleon had called him that. Could this information have come from the one-armed coachman working at Bullock's Museum? Or was Ali given that name by the show's promoters in London? Did they swap a simple Egyptian name for a dramatic, melodious European name with echoes of battle?

After a few months of cross-checking horses, their sizes, coats, colours, dates of arrival in the imperial stables and provenance, I felt I could probably surmise that Marengo was Ali or Aly – either spelling is used. Of all the Emperor's horses, he is the most distinguished contender. An Arab, he was in the First Consul's stables before the

214

imperial stables were established, he was a dirty grey colour and his height is spot on. But there are two main differences between the supposed lives of Ali and Marengo.

When Marengo was exhibited in London, he was advertised as wearing the saddle that he had worn in Russia, having walked over 3,000 miles to Moscow and back, but Ali was at a stud in Normandy and did not take part in the Russian campaign. Inaccuracies like this surround many of Napoleon's horses. (At times during the research it seemed as if the attributes of all Napoleon's personal horses were embodied in that one animal in London.) Apart from the Russian campaign, Marengo was advertised as having been at all the same battles as Ali.

The second main difference between Ali and Marengo is age, but perhaps the estimated ages for both horses were incorrect. When captured in 1799 Marengo was supposed to have been six or seven years old, whereas Ali was said to have been born in 1799, though there could have been a confusion between the year of his capture and his birth. Six or seven years difference is a lot for a horse, but both ages were only estimates. In one article Marengo is referred to as the doyen of the imperial stables, but there are few horses of any stature which preceded Ali. If he was born in 1799 no horses could have preceded him. According to Hesse's drawing, which also places Ali's birth around 1799, there is an inconsistency in age. Marengo was supposed to have been born in 1792 or 1793, but on Hesse's drawing Ali is stated to be ten years old in 1809. However, despite apparent differences, Ali is still the closest match to the elusive Marengo. He was indeed one of Napoleon's favourites. One other clue was provided by Stephen Wood, the Keeper of the Scottish United Services Museum in Edinburgh Castle, who used to work at the National Army Museum. He said that a vet, on inspecting Marengo's skeleton, had told him that the bones in the spine where the saddle had once rested were distorted. He had been ridden when too young, when the bones were too soft.

All these contradictions fuel the myth of Marengo. As original riddles were solved, new ones appeared. True successor to Pegasus, Marengo seemed a mixture of myth and fact. Was he, indeed, another horse? Whatever the truth, Marengo seems to have adapted well to living in three different countries, the country of his birth, France and England. He also responded to at least three different names: his first name; the name he received when he first entered Napoleon's personal stable after Aboukir; and the magic name 'Marengo', which he may have received, in fact, in England.

When someone suggested that a possible solution to some of the riddles might be DNA testing on the remains, the quest for Marengo's fourth hoof took on a new urgency. Scientific experts at Newmarket said that such tests required only a little tissue left inside one of the hooves. Even though there seemed little that such a test could prove, I decided to pursue it and, after two paragraphs about the hoof appeared in the *Daily Mail* gossip column in July 1999, a postcard led to its discovery. A horse-breeder put me in contact with the widow of a descendant of J. J. Angerstein, who runs a bed and breakfast farmhouse near Wincanton in Somerset. The hoof – with its inscribed silver lid and a handful of Marengo's mane – was hidden in a plastic bag in a drawer. As she rushed the hoof off to a bank safety deposit box, she made me promise never to reveal her identity. But neither this hoof nor the other three contained enough tissue for DNA testing.

The Napoleon legend continued to grow after his exile to St Helena, fuelled by the publication of Emmanuel de Las Cases's *Mémorial de Sainte-Hélène*, which accused the English of causing his death and accentuated his 'martyrdom on the rock'. Because Marengo's very name was redolent of Napoleon's victories in Italy and the heyday of *La Gloire*, once in England details about the imperial horse became distorted, merging into the fantasy surrounding Napoleon.

The myth of Napoleon and the horse became fused and began to develop: Napoleon, the self-made man of action, the genius, was seen as the officer who became the all-conquering general. So great was the interest in Napoleon that even Sir Walter Scott temporarily abandoned his historical novels to write about him, and Lord Rosebery, who was briefly Prime Minister, became one of many authors to produce academic histories and best-selling books on Britain's former foe. They were joined by the likes of Byron, Stendhal, Goethe, Balzac, Alfred de Vigny, Alfred de Musset, Pushkin, Heine, Manzoni, Dostoevsky, Thackeray, Rudyard Kipling, Walter de la Mare, George Bernard Shaw and others. Chateaubriand's remark about Napoleon was fulfilled: 'Living he lost the world, dead he conquers it.' Victor Hugo portrayed Napoleon often as the hero on horseback who, with his superbly trained cavalry and great daring, could always surpass himself at a push; and the horse, with its strength and its speed, was part of his might. Paintings also fuelled the myth. Napoleon was shown mounted on beautifully groomed white horses. Artists like Ingres, as well as artists who had never cast eyes on Napoleon, painted him. Jean-Louis Meissonier produced seven such canvases. Later Toulouse-Lautrec painted a striking poster of Napoleon on a white horse for an exhibition in Paris in 1895, which shows him with his aide-de-camp and his turbaned Mameluke servant in billowing silk pantaloons. The aide-de-camp's head in the background is blurred, but the other three are given equal importance, proving that the legend of the white horse remained potent. Indeed, the face of the horse was as important as that of the rider. Among the many inspirations for the poster were two works by Victor Hugo. In *Les Misérables* Hugo describes Napoleon with 'the white horse with his housings of purple velvet with crowned Ns and eagles on the corners'. In his poem 'Les Châtiments' the horses speak:

Napoleon on St Helena, taking one of his rare walks around the coast of the island. The painting is by an anonymous soldier.

Le cheval de bataille alors, plein de fureur,
Indigné, bien pensant, dit: 'Vive l'empereur!'

[The battle horse, then, full of fury
Angry, but thinking straight, says 'Long live the Emperor!']

In London, many popular items, such as the mass-produced aquatint of Napoleon on a fiery horse by the edge of a shaggy cliff on St Helena, were first printed. That caption read:

Bonaparte takes much exercise on Horseback, and frequently rides up those mountainous precipices which strikes the beholder with terror – in the excursion above represented, the officer (Captain Thomas Poppleton) in attendance, prudently chose a circuitous route.

Although fat, ill, in his late forties and out of condition, Napoleon was still intrepid. His competence was unexpected, as Sir Hudson Lowe reported that Napoleon had not ridden for four years before May 1820.

Books, cartoons and prints fuelled the Napoleonic myth and merged speculation with fiction. Marengo responded well to being in the limelight. He became emblematic of the many horses used by Napoleon and acquired legendary characteristics. As Napoleon's fame grew, he continued to stride, ride and gallop off imposing canvases. In many reproductions of paintings and lithographs, the Emperor was depicted on a pale grey or white horse which looked very much like Marengo. So when he was on display in London he was thought to be the very mount in many of these illustrations, even though a number of other horses were used as models. Marengo, for many people, was Napoleon's one and only horse. And the publications were so numerous that today the London Library has over 3,000 books about Napoleon, yet only a small shelf is devoted to works about Wellington. All have fuelled the myth of Napoleon and, indirectly, that of Marengo.

Major-General W. Tweedie in his respected book *The Arabian Horse*, published at the end of the nineteenth century, foresaw the problems of trying to untangle the riddle of Napoleon's horses: 'the chronicler is unborn who can unfold the histories of his Marengo, Marie, Austerlitz, Ali and Jaffa, all of whom were grey or white in colour. All that can be certainly said on this point is that a white Arab became part of the Napoleonic legend.'

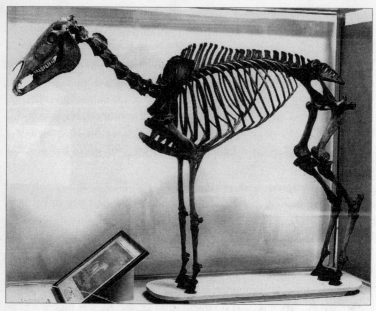

Marengo's skeleton at the National Army Museum,
with two hooves missing.

When Hitler arranged for the remains of Napoleon's son to be moved to Paris in 1940 and buried beside Napoleon's tomb at Les Invalides, the imperial stuffed horse sent to France by the Manchester Natural History Society was already on show less than a hundred yards away at the Musée de l'Armée, along with the imperial tented bed and exhibits recalling Napoleon's victories and defeats. Today a placard says that he is Vizir, one of the French horses which accompanied Napoleon to St Helena. Dr Godefroy de la Roche concluded that it is most likely that 'the horse displayed in Les Invalides is not Vizir, but he has become so by the force of habit.

Anyway it looks like him so let us leave him in peace so that the thousands of visitors who stop, sometimes amused, sometimes emotional, do so in front of the Horse of Napoleon.'

The exploits credited to Marengo may be hard to believe, but he was known to have belonged to and have been ridden by Napoleon. A further question remains, though. Did Napoleon really have a favourite charger? Was it Marengo? Was it Vizir? Was it the first or the second Roitelet? Or was it Ali? Or all of them? Perhaps it is best to leave the mystery unsolved so the thousands of sightseers who yearly visit Marengo in England and Vizir in France can, through them, honour each and every horse who played a part in the large odyssey of Napoleon's cavalry. The fiery stallion in the famous canvas *Napoleon Crossing the Alps* by Jacques Louis David is not just one horse, but a composite. Indeed, this horse is the very spirit of Napoleon himself. He is Pegasus, unconfined by time or space.

Brief Chronology

1768   The island of Corsica becomes French.

1769   *15 August:* Napoleon born in Ajaccio, Corsica.

1774   Louis XVI ascends the throne of France.

1775   American War of Independence.

1779   *15 May:* Napoleon enters military school in Brienne, in the Champagne district of France.

1784   *22 May:* enters military school in Paris.

1785   *February:* death of his father Charles Bonaparte.
November: joins La Fère regiment.

1786   *September:* returns to Ajaccio for a year.

1787   *October:* travels from Ajaccio to Paris.

1788   *January:* second visit to Ajaccio.
June: joins his garrison in Auxonne.

1789   Storming of the Bastille; the French Revolution; Declaration of the Rights of Man.
September: returns to Corsica for fifteen months. Troubles in Ajaccio.

1790   Abolition of titles and nobility by Constituent Assembly; Pasquale Paoli returns to Corsica from London.

1791   *January:* Napoleon returns to regiment in Auxonne; tries to find publisher for his *Histoire de la Corse*; arrest of Louis XVI and family at Varennes.
September: Napoleon makes fourth return to Corsica.

1792   Returns to France; goes to Paris where he witnesses the insurrections of 20 June and 10 August; France declares war on Austria; incarceration of Louis XVI; abolition of royalty in France. *September:* French Republic declared.
October: Napoleon returns to Corsica.

1793   Louis XVI guillotined; Britain declares war on France; breaks with Paoli; the whole Bonaparte family escapes from Corsica and flees to Toulon; execution of Marie Antoinette.
December: Napoleon leads the Siege of Toulon; promoted to general of the brigade.

1794   Involved in various military operations in northern Italy.
27 July/9 Thermidor: Fall of Robespierre; end of Reign of Terror; Napoleon arrested for two weeks due to his friendship with Augustin Robespierre.

1795   The Directoire made the executive authority in France.
5 October/13 Vendémiaire: crushes the Royalist riots in Paris; made general in chief of the Army of the Interior.

1796   *March:* marriage to Josephine de Beauharnais in Paris; made General of the Army of Italy; leads campaign against the Austrians in northern Italy; victories at Montenotte, Millesimo, Dego, Mondovi, Lodi, Lonato, Castiglione, Roveredo, Bassano, Saint-Georges and Arcole.

1797   Victory at Rivolio; Peace of Campoformio.

1798   Egyptian campaign: Battle of the Pyramids; enters Cairo.
July: Nelson's victory at the Battle of the Nile; conquest of upper Egypt.

1799   Campaign in Syria: victories at El-Alrich and Jaffa; defeated at Saint-Jean d'Acre; victory at Aboukir Bay where Marengo is said to have been captured.
August: returns to France leaving his army in Egypt.
November: coup d'état of *18 Brumaire*; becomes one of the three consuls who govern France and on 12 December

becomes First Consul; starts to improve and expand all cavalry
units.

1800 *June:* crosses St Bernard pass; Battle of Marengo – reconquers
northern Italy; establishes Bank of France.

1801 *February:* Treaty of Lunéville with Austria.

August: French in Egypt surrender to British; Britain acquires the
Rosetta stone.

1802 Peace of Amiens means that the British flock to Paris; Concordat
with the Papacy; Napoleon elected Consul-for-Life; armistice
given to émigrés.

1803–4 Napoleon establishes the new Civil Code in France which is later
adopted in much of Europe.

1803 End of peace with Britain; Britain declares war on France; sale of
Louisiana to the United States; Napoleon visits Boulogne to
observe the English coast in preparation for an invasion of
England.

1804 The duc d'Enghien is shot dead; the Empire is proclaimed and
Napoleon made Emperor of the French.

December: coronation ceremony at Notre-Dame celebrated by the
Pope.

1805 Becomes King of Italy; Third Coalition (England, Russia,
Austria); the Grand Army moved from Boulogne to Germany.

October: victories at Elchingen and Ulm; Nelson's victory in the
sea battle off Cape Trafalgar destroys France's hopes of naval
supremacy; plans to invade England crushed.

December: victory over the Austrians and Russians at Austerlitz.

1806 Joseph Bonaparte made King of the Two Sicilies and Louis
Bonaparte made King of Holland; the Confederation of the
Rhine is created; Prussia joins the Coalition but Napoleon
crushes them with his victory at Jena; occupation of Berlin and
the north of Germany; economic war declared on Britain with
the continental blockade.

1807   Defeat of Russians at Friedland by the French; Treaty of Tilsit with Tsar.

October: France invades Portugal.

1808   Joseph Bonaparte made King of Spain; Spanish rise against French occupation of Spain; beginning of Peninsular War; French campaign against the British in Spain.

1809   Invasion of Portugal by the French; annexation of the Papal States and imprisonment of the Pope; Fifth Coalition against France; occupation of Vienna.

May: Battle of Essling.

July: victory at Wagram.

October: peace between France and Austria; Napoleon's need for an heir leads to official divorce with Josephine.

1810   Marries Marie Louise, daughter of the Emperor of Austria; war continued in Spain.

1811   *20 March:* birth at the Tuileries of Napoleon's only legitimate son, later King of Naples.

1812   Crosses the Niemen to invade Russia; Battle of Borodino; French occupation of Moscow which the Russians ignite; disastrous retreat.

1813   Sixth Coalition against France.

May to October: campaign in Germany; victories for Napoleon at Lützen, Bautzen and Bresden, but defeated at Leipzig; British victory in Spain led by Wellesley; flight of Joseph Bonaparte.

October: Wellesley crosses the Pyrenees.

November: Wellesley advances into France.

1814   Battles in France – victories include Champaubert, Montmirail, de Château-Thierry, de Vauchamp, de Montereau; defeated at D'Arcis-sur-Aube; the Allies led by the Tsar march into Paris; Napoleon abdicates; exiled to the island of Elba; Wellesley created Duke of Wellington.

29 May: death of Josephine; Louis XVIII, brother of the late

Louis XVI, returns to Paris; Wellington appointed British Ambassador to France.

1815 Escapes from Elba and lands at Golfe Juan on 1 March; the Hundred Days commence; Napoleon reclaims his rooms at the Tuileries; Wellington appointed Commander of the Anglo-Netherland and Hanoverian forces.

16 June: the French attack battle at Ligny, Napoleon's last victory.

18 June: Battle of Waterloo.

21 June: Napoleon reaches Paris.

22 June: abdicates for a second time.

15 July: surrenders to the British, and is exiled to the island of St Helena in the Atlantic where he arrives in October; meanwhile the white terror against supporters of the Revolution, Napoleon or the Empire; Treaty of Paris signed by France.

1821 *5 May:* death on St Helena.

Acknowledgements

I am extremely grateful to the many people in France, England and Australia who have made this book possible and I commence my long list of thanks with Her Majesty, Queen Elizabeth II, for permission to use material from the Royal Archives in Windsor, and the staff and officers at the Officers' Mess at St James's Palace for welcoming me there to inspect and photograph Marengo's hoof.

Space does not allow me to name everyone, but I must first acknowledge a great debt of gratitude to Joelle Fleming whose research and translations have helped to shape this book. Her insights during six months of research have been remarkable. The book was to be dedicated to her, but we both decided it should be a tribute to 'all horses, in all wars'. The central source of research has been the 1992 thesis by Dr Godefroy de la Roche, *Les Chevaux de Napoleon I et les Écuries Impériales*. Many thanks go to him for allowing me to share his research and to the Musée de l'Armée for guiding me to this and to Philipe Osché, who has spent two years researching into Napoleon and his horses. A bouquet of thanks goes to Rosanne Dobson who not only found Marengo's fourth hoof, but who injected much enthusiasm into the quest for Marengo and acted as a scout on the intricate trail of this elusive horse.

I could never have succeeded in pulling all the strands together without the constant and patient help of Jane Dorrell in Chelsea, and Maureen Sherriff, my neighbour on Magnetic Island. The painstaking work by Nadia Grimoult in the archives in Paris has formed much of the book's foundations, as has research by Emma Hicks in London. And, of course, thanks go to my mentor Dame Miriam Rothschild.

I especially want to thank Captain David Horn, the curator of the Guards' Museum, for giving invaluable support, Colonel Michel Perrodon, the French Army Attaché, and, of course, Robert Brain, whose early editing helped pull the book together. Alan Ventress, the librarian at the Mitchell Library in Sydney, kept a steady supply of information and encouragement going and John Montgomery, the librarian at the Royal United Services Institute was like a detective in finding vital links in the story. And, as always, Anthony Mockler has lent a guiding hand in many ways. The help given by Lady Rose – Dorothy Carrington – in Corsica has animated Napoleon's childhood. Another neighbour in Chelsea, Tom Pocock, has again given much guidance over all the naval history. Elizabeth Bancroft put much enthusiasm into the quest for Jaffa in Kent, as did Dr John Marsden of the Linnean Society, who also tracked down Vizir through Henry McGhie at the Manchester Museum. Christopher Logue gave invaluable direction in the story of the Napoleonic legend, as did Digby Neave. And I especially thank Dr Jean-François Lemaire, who won the Grand Prix in 1999 from the Fondation Napoléon, for reading the final manuscript.

The happiest times in my life have been in libraries or in bookshops and some of the most enjoyable while writing this book have been at the London Library; the Library of James Cook University, Townsville; the State Library of New South Wales; the Mitchell Library; the Townsville General Library; the Chelsea Library; the library of the National Army Museum; the British Library in Bloomsbury; and the Guildhall Library, London. Without the resources at the Musée de l'Armée, the Bibliothèque Nationale and the Archive National in Paris this book would not have been possible. I would like to say what a pleasure it was to use the electronic retrieval system in the Archive Nationale. Victor Sutcliffe, the bookdealer, helped find obscure books.

I must also convey gratitude to the following for their advice, technical expertise and support: Edward Foster of the Royal United Services Museum; Professor Ross Steele; Dr Keith Harrison; Barry Delves at Hatchard's; Penny Hart, who helps me with *Flora-for-Fauna*; Dr Bernard Chevallier, the curator at Malmaison; Liz Leighton-Jones; Atalanta Clifford; Count Charles de Salis; Lord Petre; Jane Allen; Colonel Don Murray; Emily Hayward; Arthur MacGregor; Professor Ruthven Blackburn; Margot Creedy; Penny Olsen;

Acknowledgements

Professor Don Gallagher; the Arab Horse Society; Wayne Harrison; Rosemary Archer; and Ian Fleming. There is, alas, not room to list all the people who helped and guided me on this long trail. I would also like to extend a special word of thanks to Christopher Potter, the publisher, who gave me the idea of writing this book, and, of course, Janet Law who edited the typescript.

I am particularly grateful for all the research that Proctor Jones has done on Napoleon and for producing his excellent book, *Napoleon: How He Did It*, on Napoleon's secretary, Baron Fain. The book has been much helped by his quotes from Baron Fain on horses. Quotations from the works of Rudyard Kipling by permission of A. P. Watt Ltd on behalf of The National Trust for Places of Historic Interest or Natural Beauty.

Photo Credits

Thanks to the following for providing illustrations:

p.x. Author's collection. p.5. Courtesy of Rosanne Dobson. p.7. The Wallace Collection, London, UK/Bridgeman Art Library. p.13. Author's collection. p.16. Musée d'Art et d'Histoire, Palais Massena/Photograph by Michael de Lorenzo. p.26. Réunion des Musées Nationaux/Louvre. p.28. Author's collection. p.29 & 41. Musée d'Art et d'Histoire, Palais Massena/Photograph by Michael de Lorenzo. p.88. London Library. p.109. Courtesy of the Morrab Library, Penzance. p.114. The Bridgeman Art Library/Château de Versailles, France. p.124, 128 & 131. Réunion des Musées Nationaux/Château de Versailles. p.134. Boulogne-Billancourt, Bibliothèque MarmottanGiraudon. p.156. Musée d'Orsay/Giraudon. p.185. Courtesy of the Morrab Library, Penzance. p.198. Bodleian Library, Oxford/John Johnson Collection. p.202. City of Westminster Archive Centre/Bridgeman Art Library. p.204. Christie's Images/Bridgeman Art Library. p.218. Lancashire Fusiliers Museum. p.220. By Courtesy of the National Army Museum.

Every effort has been made to contact the copyright holders. Please contact the publishers in the event that information has been omitted.

Bibliography

It would be impossible to list all the books consulted. An indication of the extent of printed matter on Napoleon, let alone Josephine, can be seen in the catalogue at the London Library which lists well over 3,000 books. Instead I have listed those books which have been particularly useful or for which I have developed a special affection. (The dates are of first publication.)

Manuscript Sources

Archives Nationale, Paris – 0^2 76 à 84 *Ordres de Services pour les écuries an XIII – 1809 – noms des chevaux; achats de chevaux et voitures, etc.*, 0^2 85 et 86; 0^2 108 et 109

Bibliothèque, Musee de l'Armée, Paris: de la Roche, Dr Godefroy, *Les Chevaux de Napoleon I et les Ecuries Impériales* (Paris, 1992)

Westminster City Archives Department (Poor Rates, Street Directories, Trade Directories)

Bodleian Library, Oxford, John Johnson collection

Royal Archives, Windsor Castle (RA/GEO 26517)

Royal United Services Institute for Defence Studies, London

The Guards' Museum, Wellington Barracks, London

National Army Museum Library

Cranbrook Library, Kent

Probate Department, Principal Registry of Family Division, London

National Register of Archives, London

Weatherby's, Northants.: Eclipse Pedigrees/Stud Book Division

Arab Horse Society, Ramsbury, Wiltshire.

Memorialists on St Helena

Abell, Mrs Lucia Elizabeth (formerly Betsy Balcombe), *Recollections of the Emperor Napoleon During the First Three Years of his Captivity on the Island of St Helena* (John Murray, London, 1844)

Antommarchi, Francesco, *The Last Days of the Emperor Napoleon* (Henry Colburn, London, 1825)

Bertrand, Henri-Gratien, *Napoleon at St Helena: Memoirs of General Bertrand* (Cassell, London, 1953)

Gourgaud, General Gaspard, *Journal inédit de 1815 à 1818* (Flammarion, Paris, 1899)

Las Cases, Marquis de, *Le Mémorial de Sainte-Hélène* (Garnier Frères, Paris, 1823)

Marchand, Louis Joseph Narcisse, Comte, *In Napoleon's Shadow* (Proctor Jones, San Francisco, 1998)

Montholon, Général Comte Jean-François, *Récits de la captivité de l'Empereur à Sainte Hélène* (Paulin, Paris, 1847)

O'Meara, Barry E., *Napoleon at St Helena* (Richard Bentley & Son, London, 1888)

Selected Reading List

Abrantès, Duchesse d' (Madame Junot), *Memoirs*, 4 vols (Albin Michel, Paris, n.d.)

d'Arblay, Madame, *The Diaries and Letters of Madame d'Arblay*, vol. VI, *1793–1812* (Henry Colburn, London, 1854)

Barras, Paul-François, *Memoirs*, ed. George Duruy, 4 vols (Osgood McIlvaine, London, 1895–6)

Bergeron, Louis, *France Under Napoleon* (Princeton University Press, New Jersey, 1972)

Blaine, Delabere, *Encyclopaedia of Rural Sports* (Longman, Orme & co., London, 1840)

Blond, Georges, *La Grande Armée* (Arms & Armour, London, 1979)

Bourrienne, Louis Antoine, *Memoirs*, 4 vols (Constable, London, 1831)

Brereton, J. M., *The Horse in War* (Newton Abbot: David & Charles, 1976)

Brett-James, Antony, *The British Soldier in the Napoleonic Wars 1793–1815* (Macmillan, London, 1970)

Brett-James, Antony, *1812 Eyewitness Accounts of Napoleon's Defeat in Russia* (Macmillan, London, 1966)

Brookes, Dame Mabel, *St Helena Story* (Heinemann, London, 1960)

Bryant, Arthur, *The Years of Endurance 1793–1802* (Collins, London, 1942)

Carlyle, Thomas, *The French Revolution* (Chapman & Hall, London, 1900)

Carrington, Dorothy, *Napoleon and His Parents* (Viking, New York, 1988); *Napoléon et ses parents* (Viking, New York, 1988); *Napoléon et ses parents*, (Editions Alain Pazzola & La Marge, Ajaccio)

——*Granite Island* (Longmans, London, 1971)

Castelot, André, *Napoleon* (Harper & Row, New York, 1971)

——*Bonaparte* (Librairie Académique Perrin, Paris, 1967)

Caulaincourt, General Armand de, *Mémoires*, trans. Hamish Miles and George Libaire, 2 vols, 1935–38.

——*Mémoires de la campagne de Russie l'agonie de Fontainebleau presentation et choix de texts par André Castelot* (Librairie académique Perrin, Paris, 1986)

Chandler, David, *The Campaigns of Napoleon* (Weidenfeld & Nicolson, London, 1993)

——*On the Napoleonic Wars* (Greenhill Books, London, 1994)

Charles-Roux, F., *Bonaparte: Governor of Egypt* (Methuen, London, 1937)

Chevallier, Bernard, Maurice Catinat and Christophe Pincemaille, *L'impératrice Joséphine – Correspondance, 1782–1814* (Editions Payot & Rivages, Paris, 1996)

Constant, *Memoirs of Constant, the Emperor Napoleon's Head Valet, Containing Details of the Private Life of Napoleon, His Family and His Court*, ed. L.C. Wairy (Chez Bechet, Paris, 1820; London, 1896)

Cronin, Vincent, *Napoleon* (Collins, London, 1971)

De Chair, Somerset, *Napoleon on Napoleon* (Cassell, London, 1991)

de la Tour du Pin, Madame, *Memoirs* (Harvill Press, London, 1969)

Detaille, Edouard, *L'Armée Française* (Waxtel & Hasenauer, Quantum Printing Company, New York, 1992)

Dixon, Pierson, *Pauline, Napoleon's Favourite Sister* (Collins, London, 1964)

Duffy, Christopher, *Austerlitz* (Cassell, London, 1977)

Dziewanowski, M. K., *Alexander I: Russia's Mysterious Tsar* (Hippocrene Books, New York, 1990)

Etling, John R., *Swords Around a Throne: Napoleon's Grande Armée* (Phoenix Giant, London, 1989)

Fain, Baron, *Napoleon: How He Did It* (Proctor Jones, San Francisco, 1998)

Fussell, G. E., *James Ward R.A.* (Michael Joseph, London, 1974)

Gaussen, Dominique & Henry Patrick, *Napoléon et Son Temps* (Mango, Paris, 1994)

Goodspeed, D. J., *Bayonets at St Cloud* (Rupert Hart-Davis, London, 1964)

Haitley Edwards, Elwyn, *Encylopaedia of the Horse* (Dorling Kindersley, London, 1994)

Hall, H. F., *Napoleon's Letters to Josephine* (J. M. Dent, London, 1901)

Hamilton, Jill, Duchess of, *Napoleon, the Empress and the Artist* (Kangaroo Press, Sydney, 1999)

Haythornthwaite, Philip J., *Who Was Who in the Napoleonic Wars* (Arms & Armour, London, 1998)

Holland, Henry Holland Fox, Fourth Baron, *Journal, 1818–30* (Thornton Butterworth, London, 1923)

Hortense, Queen, *The Memoirs of Queen Hortense*, ed. J. Hanoteau (New York, 1927); *Mémoires de la reine Hortense, publiée par le prince Napoléon* (Paris, Plon, n.d.)

Hugo, Victor, *Les Miserables* (Penguin, London, 1980)

Johnson, David, *Napoleon's Cavalry and Its Leaders* (Spellmount, Staplehurst, 1999)

Jones, Proctor Patterson, *Napoleon: An Intimate Account of the Years of Supremacy* (Proctor Jones, San Francisco, 1992)

Kerry, Earl of, *The First Napoleon* (Houghton Mifflin, Boston and New York, 1925)

Keynes, Milo, 'The Medical Health of Napoleon Bonaparte', *Journal of Medical Biography*, 8(1996), 108–17

La campagne d'Egypte, *Mythes et Réalités* from the conference of that name, June 1998 (Editions In Forma, Paris, 1998)

Longford, Elizabeth, *Wellington: The Years of the Sword* (Weidenfeld & Nicolson, London, 1969)

——*Wellington: Pillar of State* (Weidenfeld & Nicolson, London, 1972)

Luvaas, Jay, *Napoleon on the Art of War* (The Free Press, New York, 1999)

McLynn, Frank, *Napoleon* (Jonathan Cape, London, 1997)

Malcolm, Lady Clementia, *A Diary of St Helena, 1816, 1817* (Allen & Unwin, London, 1929)

Martineau, Gilbert, *Napoleon Surrenders* (John Murray, London, 1971)

Mercer, General, *Journal of the Waterloo Campaign* (Greenhill Books, London, 1985)

Meneval, Claude-François, Baron de, *Memoirs to Serve for the History of Napoleon I from 1802 to 1815* (Hutchinson, London, 1894)

Nicolson, Harold, *The Congress of Vienna* (Constable, London, 1948)

Oman, Carola, *Britain Against Napoleon* (Faber & Faber, London, 1940)

Bibliography

Palmer, Alan, *An Encyclopaedia of Napoleon's Europe* (Constable, London, 1984)

Pocock, Tom, *A Thirst for Glory: The Life of Admiral Sir Sidney Smith* (Pimlico, London, 1998)

Pope, Stephen, *The Cassell Dictionary of the Napoleonic Wars* (Cassell, London, 1999)

Rémusat, Madame de, *Mémoires, 1802–8*, ed. Calman Lévy, 3 vols (Michael Lévy, Paris, 1893)

Rosebery, Lord, *Napoleon: The Last Phase* (Arthur L. Humphreys, London, 1900)

Saunders, Edith, *The Hundred Days* (Longman, London, 1964)

Schom, Alan, *Napoleon Bonaparte* (HarperCollins, London, 1997)

Seth-Smith, Michael, *The Horse in Art and History* (New English Library, London, 1978)

Shankland, Peter, *Beware of Heroes* (William Kimber, London, 1975)

Staël, Madame de, *Ten Years Exile* (Centaur Press, Fontwell, 1968)

Strawson, John, *The Duke and the Emperor* (Constable, London, 1994)

Thompson, J. M., *Napoleon's Letters* (Prion Books, London, 1934)

Thrasher, Peter Adam, *Pasquale Paoli an Enlightened Hero, 1725–1807* (Constable, London 1970)

Tolstoy, Leo, *War and Peace* (Penguin, London, 1957)

Tweedie, Major-General William, *The Arabian Horse* (Blackwood, Edinburgh, 1894)

Vachée, Colonel, *Napoléon en campagne* (Paris, 1913); trans. as *Napoleon at Work* (A. & C. Black, London, 1914)

Wain, John, *The Journals of James Boswell, 1761–95* (Heinemann, London, 1990).

Walker, Stella, in *The Horseman's Companion* (Country Life, London, 1954)

Wilson-Smith, Timothy, *Napoleon and His Artists* (Constable, London, 1996)

Wood, Stephen, *The Scottish Soldier* (National Museums of Scotland, Edinburgh, 1987)

Index